shakespeare **made clear**

A Midsummer Night's Dream

A MODERN DAY TRANSLATION

shakespeare **made clear**

A Midsummer Night's Dream

A MODERN DAY TRANSLATION

BELMONT
PRESS

shakespeare made clear

Love. Lust. Sex. Jealousy. Violence. Vengeance. Tyranny. From *Hamlet* to *Macbeth* to *Romeo and Juliet*, the subjects William Shakespeare brought to life in blank verse and rhyme are just as relevant today as they were when his plays were first performed more than four hundred years ago. But if Shakespeare's themes are timeless, the same thing can't be said about his centuries-old texts.

You already know some of Shakespeare's most famous turns of phrase. "Friends, Romans, countrymen, lend me your ears" (*Julius Caesar*). "The world's mine oyster"(*The Merry Wives of Windsor*). "The wheel is come full circle" (*King Lear*). "To be, or not to be: that is the question" (*Hamlet,* of course). But most of the time Shakespeare's Elizabethan English looks and sounds like a foreign language to modern eyes and ears—and if you've ever tried reading Shakespeare on your own, you probably tossed the play aside and said, "It was Greek to me" (*Julius Caesar* again).

That's where the Shakespeare Made Clear series comes in. If you can read and understand modern American English, you can read and understand Shakespeare's plays in these effectively bilingual editions from Belmont Press.

On every page of every play, Shakespeare's original text is followed by an up-to-date, line-by-line "translation," in a clean, streamlined design that eliminates confusion and puts everything you need right in front of you. And Shakespeare Made Clear doesn't stop with modernizing the language of the plays. Many pages of each play feature insights into Shakespeare's original text, whether they involve historical facts, local color, the origins of an unusual word or phrase, or a character's deeper motives. Each play also includes an introductory discussion of the play's dramatic structure, its origins and historical context, and its various versions and adaptations. At the end of the play, there are summaries of every scene as well as lively, nuanced discussions about the characters and themes— and about the author, of course.

Shakespeare Made Clear. Because there's no good reason to struggle with the language when "the play's the thing" (*Hamlet*).

Contents

Appendix 3
Appendix 4

Introduction

Scholars can and do argue endlessly about which of Shakespeare's comedies is his best. The usual contenders are *As You Like It*, *Twelfth Night*, and *The Tempest*. *A Midsummer Night's Dream* doesn't even make the cut.

For hundreds of years, the play was dismissed as a piece of fluff, a mere pretext for onstage song and dance. In 1662, for example, its "insipid" and "ridiculous" nature was lamented by the English diarist Samuel Pepys (rhymes with "weeps"), although Pepys did confess that he enjoyed the play's "good dancing" and "handsome" women. And it's true that many aspects of *A Midsummer Night's Dream* are silly, even ridiculous, as Pepys charged. After all, the play features mixed-up lovers and mischievous fairies, not to mention a plot that calls on the cast to portray a company of ham actors.

But in recent decades, admiration has been growing for the play specifically as a piece of writing. Shakespeare weaves the comedy's three groups of characters together so neatly, and ties up its themes so tightly, that closer inspection reveals the play to be a masterwork of dramatic structure. It also contains some of Shakespeare's most beautiful poetry and presents some of his most memorable characters. In no other play by Shakespeare is there anyone as wild as Puck or as funny as Bottom, and his work offers few other scenes as riotous as the fight involving Hermia, Helena, Lysander, and Demetrius or as comical as the rehearsal and play staged by the "rude mechanicals" (a group of tradesmen). Some of Shakespeare's other plays are certainly greater, deeper, and more important. But as pure romantic comedy, *A Midsummer Night's Dream* sets a high bar, one that no one has topped in four hundred years.

Nevertheless, when a modern-day student opens a standard copy of this comedy, one question usually comes to mind: "*This* is supposed to be *funny*?" Well, yes. It is supposed to be funny, and it actually is funny. But you wouldn't know that today, because the play was written in a way that would make immediate sense if you had a pair of sixteenth-century ears, and yours are younger than that. In addition, much of the hilarity is buried in jokes that haven't made sense since the 1590s, and in words that were normal then but might as well be in a foreign language now (which is pretty much how your grandchildren will probably describe the way *you* talk only fifty years from now). What's most difficult of all is that *A Midsummer Night's Dream* is outrageously funny when you see it performed, but the play's comedy is so visual and so physical that it can be hard for a reader to understand what's going on.

And that's where this edition of the play comes to the rescue. In these pages you'll find the original text, a "translation" of the text into modern English, and notes that explain unfamiliar words and jokes and highlight important themes and ideas. As you read, imagine the scenes being performed in a theater. Let your mind's eye show you the silliest kind of slapstick, and you'll be on the right track. And when you've finished reading, you'll understand and probably like this play enough to look for it onstage, or at least on video. After all, that's why Shakespeare wrote *A Midsummer Night's Dream*—so it could be performed and make people laugh, even twenty-first-century people like you.

About the Play

A comedy was easily defined in the ancient world of the Greek dramatists—it had a happy ending, preferably with lovers getting married. And *A Midsummer Night's Dream* more than fits that classical definition, since the end of the play has three couples getting married and one feuding couple being reunited. But the play also fits the mold of a Shakespearean romantic comedy, which typically includes the following elements:

- Love as the main topic
- Obstacles that lovers must overcome on their way to happiness
- Supernatural or fantastic people, places, or things (fairies, enchanted forests, idealistic visions of places)
- Strange or unlikely events (mistaken identity mix-ups, improbable meetings, nobles falling for commoners)
- Subthemes other than love (transformation, appearances versus reality, the importance of art and poetry, the power of dreams)

Dramatic Structure

Just as *A Midsummer Night's Dream* meets the classical definition of a comedy, the play's dramatic structure meets the classical definition of a theatrical work, whether comedy or tragedy. By this definition, a dramatic work must include five elements: an exposition, rising action, a climax, falling action, and a conclusion.

The beginning of the play is the *exposition*. This is where the scene is set and the major characters are introduced. As *A Midsummer Night's Dream* opens, Theseus and Hippolyta are planning their wedding; Hermia's father wants her to marry Demetrius, but Hermia loves Lysander and faces death or life in a nunnery if she doesn't obey her father; and meanwhile Helena is in love with Demetrius, who doesn't return her love.

The middle of the play is where the *rising action* takes place, as the main characters try to solve a problem or resolve a conflict but find more and more obstacles in their path. Here, Hermia and Lysander decide to run away together into the woods so that Hermia can escape a forced marriage to Demetrius, and Helena and Demetrius follow them. Subplots are also introduced to reflect and complicate the situation; in this case, the Mechanicals plan and rehearse their play while various other characters argue, plot, cast spells, and accidentally make the wrong people fall in love with each other. The middle of the play is also where the *climax* occurs—the moment when the plan to solve a problem or resolve a conflict either succeeds or fails. In *A Midsummer Night's Dream*, the climax occurs when—after still more arguments, spells, plots, and confusion—the pairs of lovers are correctly matched up.

At the end of the play comes the *falling action*, a term meaning everything that happens after the climax. (Another term for this part of the play is *denouement*, a French word that literally means "unknotting" or in the words of our own familiar expression, "tying up loose ends.") In this play, as already mentioned, three marriages take place (with Hermia allowed to marry the man she loves), quarrels are resolved, and spells are lifted. And at the play's *conclusion*, the happily married couples watch the play put on by the Mechanicals.

Origins

Although many of Shakespeare's plays can be traced directly to specific sources—historical events, legends, or popular poems or stories—the tangled plot of *A Midsummer Night's Dream* seems to have been hatched mostly in Shakespeare's mind. The play does contain references to a wide variety of literary works, including Plutarch's *Lives of the Noble Greeks and Romans* and "The Knight's Tale" from Geoffrey Chaucer's *The Canterbury Tales*, and its theme of transformation may well have been inspired by *Metamorphoses*, a first-century C.E. narrative poem in fifteen books by the influential Roman poet Ovid. As for the play's fairies and supernatural forest creatures that come out at night, these may have been borrowed from ancient myths about supernatural races whom people forced into hiding, and who then committed retaliatory mischief against human beings. Other likely influences include sources as diverse as country-village folklore and *Huon of Bordeaux*, a thirteenth-century epic with Romantic elements. But again, the blending of all these sources seems to be purely a product of Shakespeare's imagination.

A Midsummer Night's Dream was probably written between 1595 and 1596, around the same time as *Richard II* and *Romeo and Juliet*. Scholars have long suggested that the play was written to be performed as part of a wedding celebration at some noble house. Given the play's subject matter—love and marriage—that certainly seems like a possibility, but no real evidence has ever turned up to connect the play with a specific event.

Historical Context

In 1547, when King Henry VIII died, he was succeeded on the throne by his son, Edward VI. But Edward was just a boy when he became king. The nation knew that he was frail and under the guidance of questionable protectors, and the situation left a feeling of unease throughout the country.

Edward died in 1553, and Henry's eldest daughter Mary became queen. Under the terms of a marriage treaty, Mary was wed to Philip II of Spain, who became King of England and Ireland while Mary reigned. The two of them were passionate Catholics, eager to bring England back into the Roman Catholic fold after Henry's declaration that the country would be Protestant. Mary ordered widespread persecution of Protestants, and that action earned her the nickname "Bloody Mary."

Queen Mary died in 1558. Because she had no children, Elizabeth—Mary and Edward's half sister, and the last survivor among Henry's children—took the throne at the age of twenty-five. Elizabeth's coronation marked the beginning of a welcome period of calm for England after all the years of upheaval that had followed Henry's death. Although one of her first moves as queen was the establishment of an English Protestant church, life during Elizabeth's reign was generally peaceful. Under Elizabeth, the only foreign threat was from Spain and its invading navy, but even that came a full thirty years after Elizabeth took the throne. Once England beat back the Spanish Armada, all was well again in England.

On the domestic front, the biggest problems during Elizabeth's reign were periodic outbreaks of the plague and bouts of bad weather that decreased food production. There was considerable concern about who would succeed Elizabeth on the throne, since it was clear that the queen was not going to marry. But with most other aspects of domestic and political life at a comfortable equilibrium, there was plenty of time for England and the English to explore the world, produce art and literature, and create a vibrant theatrical culture.

Shakespeare set *A Midsummer Night's Dream* in Athens during the age of gods, goddesses, and mythological heroes. All the same, it's clear that most of the characters are less like gods, goddesses, and heroes than they are like English nobles—lords and ladies, dukes and duchesses, and other members of the Elizabethan aristocracy.

In Elizabeth's England, the nobility lived in castles in the country, and often a nobleman had several castles. (Sixteenth-century people didn't devote much time or effort to cleaning, and plumbing as we understand it today was nonexistent, so it was common for a nobleman to leave one castle when it got too dirty and let it "sweeten," or air out, while he went to live for a while in another of his castles.) The queen herself spent her summers traveling through the country, stopping to stay at the castles of local nobles. A visit from Elizabeth was an honor, but it was also terrifyingly expensive, since the nobleman had to offer the queen first-class food and entertainment—often including performances of plays—and keep it up for as long as she chose to stay. (This was by design—Elizabeth saved herself a lot of money by spending her summers in others' castles.)

The nobility also lived part-time at court with Elizabeth, and that meant spending a lot of time in London, where plays were generally seen in theaters. Because there was no theatrical lighting of the kind we use today, performances took place in outdoor theaters during the afternoon. A drawing of the Swan theater, which was often the site of performances by Shakespeare's company of players, shows a stage surrounded on each side by three levels of stalls, or private boxes, with space for an audience on the ground in front of the stage. The upper classes sat in the boxes—for them, "being seen" was a big part of going to the theater. The lowest-ranking people stood on the ground. They were known as *groundlings*, and much of Shakespeare's bawdy humor was intended to keep them happy, because otherwise they would talk back to the actors and throw anything they could grab at them. And there was plenty to throw—vendors roamed the audience, loudly offering oranges, apples, sweets, and beer throughout the performance. The nobles talked and ate throughout the performance, too, but they brought their own food. In these ways, the atmosphere in the theater had less in common with the way we silently watch plays or movies today than with what goes on at a modern sports event.

In all this commotion, the actors had to fight to be noticed. Much of the action took place directly downstage (that is, the part of the stage closest to the audience). No one had a microphone, and so the actors had to shout their lines and perform in a very physical manner so that audience members far in the back could understand what was going on. A small two-level structure upstage (that is, at the back of the stage, farthest from the audience) was used for scenes like the one in *Romeo and Juliet* where Juliet speaks to Romeo from her window. The floor of the stage had a trapdoor that allowed for special effects, such as a ghost or a demon suddenly appearing or disappearing. There weren't any sets to speak of. The actors had to use anything that was already onstage to create the atmosphere—for example, columns might double as trees in a forest. Offstage, the actors had a *tiring room*, or dressing room.

Each actor in the company had to be able to do everything. An actor might play in a tragedy one day and in a comedy the next, or he might play the lead in one production and a servant in another. And the actor was always a he—women weren't allowed onstage, and so young boys played the female roles until their voices changed (no wonder Shakespeare wrote several plays in which female characters had to disguise themselves as boys). Many actors were also expert swordsmen. The fight scenes in Shakespeare's plays were a big attraction, and the actors fought with real swords. On days when no play was being performed, actors sometimes gave sword-fighting exhibitions to pick up some extra money.

The actors were quick learners, too. They didn't get full scripts of a play. Instead, they just got separate sheets of paper with their characters' lines. If the play was a new one, they might not get their lines until a day or two before the show opened. And there was very little time for rehearsals. The title of *director* didn't exist yet, and so the actors staged the play themselves, more or less. The scripts didn't help much in that regard, either—they contained few directions other than *enter* and *exit*.

The scripts we have today of Shakespeare's plays are somewhat patched together. People began to collect them and print them in the late sixteenth century, but they didn't come directly from Shakespeare. Some were from his *foul papers*, or scrap-paper manuscripts, which people in the company probably picked up and gave to printers. Others were reconstituted from the memories of actors and stage managers, and this means they may be filled with unintended omissions or may contain changes that the actors made themselves. To make matters even more complicated, printers often made changes to suit their own purposes, such as turning a verse passage into prose to make it fit on a page, or changing punctuation as they saw fit. Luckily for us, however, *A Midsummer Night's Dream* is considered to have come directly from Shakespeare's foul papers, and so the play you are about to read is almost certainly from the pen of Shakespeare himself.

Other Versions and Adaptations

Today *A Midsummer Night's Dream* is one of Shakespeare's most frequently performed plays. It has a reputation among theater companies as a crowd pleaser that will always draw audiences, and it's so well written that it's easy to put on a good production, even with few resources. Audiences can always find something to laugh at during the play, and if nothing else works, the production by the Mechanicals usually brings the house down.

The comedy has always been popular with composers, and even straight productions of the play include music and dancing. The first known musical adaptation of the play is *The Fairy-Queen*, a 1692 work by Henry Purcell (pronounced "PURR-sul"). This adaptation is a series of musical pieces used in the performance of masques, or short scenes based on Shakespeare's play that feature music, dancing, sets, and elaborate costumes. *The Fairy-Queen* was often performed at noble houses, with members of the nobility taking part themselves just for the fun of it. In between the masques, lines from *A Midsummer Night's Dream* were read aloud rather than performed.

In 1826, the German Romantic composer Felix Mendelssohn wrote an overture for *A Midsummer Night's Dream* that was performed as a stand-alone piece, not intended to accompany any particular production of the play. The piece was very popular, and in 1843 he was invited to write a suite of incidental music (that is, music between scenes, or onstage songs and dances) for a German production of *A Midsummer Night's Dream*. You've probably heard one piece of music from that suite—Mendelssohn's "Wedding March," which is typically played as a recessional when the newly married couple walks back down the aisle (not to be confused with "The Bridal Suite," from Richard Wagner's opera *Lohengrin*, which is often played at formal weddings to accompany the bride's entrance). Later on, Mendelssohn's music was used in a number of ballets. In more recent times, the British composer Benjamin Britten wrote a full-scale opera version of *A Midsummer Night's Dream* that premiered in 1960.

There have been many stage productions of the play over the past several centuries. In the 1800s, the productions became ever more elaborate, with more fantastic sets, more intricate costumes, more music and dancing, and even live animals on occasion. One of the most famous productions of the play was staged by the German director Max Reinhardt at the Hollywood Bowl in 1934. Dirt was brought in and trees were planted to create a real forest, and a big wedding procession set to Mendelssohn's music was added between acts 4 and 5. That staged version was made into a movie in 1935, codirected by Reinhardt and William Dieterle, with a cast of the day's big Hollywood stars, many of whom had never performed Shakespeare before (and would never act in one of his plays again). Reinhardt and Dieterle's movie is still considered one of the best film versions. Another adaptation was filmed in 1999, this one directed by Michael Hoffman and starring such luminaries as Kevin Kline, Michelle Pfeiffer, Stanley Tucci, Calista Flockhart, and a pre-*Batman* Christian Bale.

Today *A Midsummer Night's Dream* takes all kinds of forms, from large-scale productions with fancy costumes and choreography to stripped-down shows with no sets and improvised music and dancing. The play is an especially popular offering at outdoor theaters during the summer months, when the magical atmosphere of a balmy evening can add to the onstage enchantment.

General Synopsis of the Play

Theseus, duke of Athens, is preparing to marry Hippolyta, queen of the Amazons, in four days. They get a visit from Egeus, an Athenian nobleman who is furious that his daughter, Hermia, won't marry Demetrius, the husband he has chosen for her, because she is in love with another young man, Lysander. Egeus asks Theseus to allow him to take advantage of an ancient law that would put Hermia to death for refusing to obey. But Theseus offers Hermia three choices—to marry Demetrius, to be executed under the law, or to enter a religious order and remain a virgin for the rest of her life—and he tells her to make up her mind within four days.

Lysander comes up with a plan—he and Hermia can run away and live with his wealthy widowed aunt outside Athens, where the law can't reach them. He and Hermia plan to meet the next night in the forest beyond the city.

Hermia's friend Helena arrives. She is bitter because Demetrius, who once loved her, is now in love with Hermia and plans to marry her. Hermia explains that she and Lysander are going to run away from Athens. Helena, hoping that Demetrius will be grateful, decides to tell him about the plan that Lysander and Hermia have made to meet in the forest.

In the meantime, the Mechanicals, a group of tradesmen from Athens, get together and discuss a play to be performed before Theseus as part of his wedding celebration. The Mechanicals, led by the boastful Nick Bottom, decide to put on a romantic tragedy, *Pyramus and Thisbe* (pronounced "PEER-uh-mus" and "THIZ-bee," or sometimes "TIZ-bee"). But their discussion shows that they have no idea what they're doing, and their play promises to be a disaster.

In the forest, meanwhile, the fairies are dealing with a major problem. Oberon, king of the fairies, is fighting with Titania, queen of the fairies, because he wants to take one of Titania's attendants, a mortal boy, for himself. Their battle has interrupted the usual fairy rituals, and the natural world has been thrown out of balance. Oberon says everything can get back to normal if Titania hands the boy over, but Titania refuses, saying he is the child of a dead friend who left him in her care.

Oberon then plots with Puck, his mischievous henchman, to put a spell on Titania with a magic flower. When juice from this flower is put on a sleeping person's eyes, he or she will fall in love with the first person or thing seen upon waking. Oberon hopes that Titania will fall for some horrible entity and give up the boy while she's under the flower's spell. While Puck is off fetching the flower, Oberon sees Demetrius insult Helena, who has followed the man she loves into the forest. When Puck returns, Oberon tells him to use some of the flower's juice on Demetrius so that he will fall in love with Helena.

Oberon finds Titania asleep and puts juice from the magic flower onto her eyes. Hermia and Lysander arrive in the forest and decide to stop and rest until daylight. Puck finds them sleeping, but he thinks they are Helena and Demetrius, and so he puts the flower's juice on Lysander's eyes. Puck leaves, and then the actual Helena and Demetrius arrive at the edge of the forest. Demetrius warns Helena not to follow him in, and he disappears into the trees. Helena follows anyway. When Lysander wakes up, he sees Helena and immediately begins showering her with declarations of love. Helena thinks he's making fun of her, and she runs off, with Lysander in pursuit. Hermia wakes up alone and goes off to find Lysander.

The Mechanicals meet in the forest, near the sleeping Titania, to rehearse their play. Puck sees them and decides to have some fun by placing an ass's head on Bottom. The rest of the Mechanicals are terrified and run away. Titania wakes up, sees Bottom, and falls madly in love with him.

Puck tells Oberon that he has made Titania fall in love with a man who has the head of an ass. Oberon is pleased until he sees Lysander chasing Helena and realizes that Puck has put the love juice on the eyes of the wrong man. He tries to solve the problem by putting the juice on the eyes of the sleeping Demetrius, who wakes up, sees Helena, and falls in love with her. Now Demetrius and Lysander are ready to fight over Helena, who thinks they're both teasing her. When Hermia arrives and discovers that Lysander now loves Helena, not her, all four of them fight until Puck, under orders from Oberon, temporarily leads them away from each other, at which point they all fall asleep. Puck then finds a second magic flower, one whose juice is supposed to break the spell from the juice of the first flower. He puts this spell-breaking juice on Lysander's eyes.

Oberon, now that he has persuaded Titania to give the boy to him, puts juice from the second flower on her eyes while she is sleeping. She wakes up and is horrified when Oberon shows her what she has been in love with. Puck removes the ass's head from the sleeping Bottom and the fairies run off as daylight approaches.

Theseus and Hippolyta, out in the woods with Egeus on the morning of their wedding day, plan to go hunting. They find the four young lovers asleep and wake them up. Lysander is now back in love with Hermia, but Demetrius remains in love with Helena. Lysander confesses that he and Hermia had been trying to run away, but otherwise the four of them have trouble remembering what has happened. Egeus wants to have Lysander arrested, but Theseus decrees that the two couples, now happy, should be married along with himself and Hippolyta. They all return to Athens for the weddings. Bottom wakes up, thinking that what happened was a dream, and he rushes off to find the rest of the Mechanicals. They are thrilled to see him and head to the palace, where they hope to perform their play.

After the weddings, Theseus speaks to Philostrate, the master of revels at his court, and asks for some entertainment. Philostrate gives him a list of possibilities, and Theseus chooses the Mechanicals' play because it sounds bad enough to be funny. And it is indeed dreadful, but the Mechanicals are glad to have a chance to perform, and the nobles enjoy laughing at them. Finally it's time for the couples to enjoy their wedding nights, and they leave. The fairies arrive to bless the house and all the marriages. Puck apologizes for any offense given by the evening's performance, and he asks the audience for applause.

shakespeare made clear

A Midsummer Night's Dream

A MODERN DAY TRANSLATION

Act 1

Act 1 Summary

Act 1 introduces two important groups of characters—the Athenians and the group of tradesmen known as the Mechanicals. It also introduces the conflict that puts the play in motion: the obstacles to love that confront Hermia, Lysander, Demetrius, and Helena, four young Athenians.

Theseus, the duke of Athens, and Hippolyta, the queen of the Amazons, are planning their wedding when they receive a visit from Egeus, an Athenian nobleman. Egeus complains that his daughter, Hermia, refuses to marry Demetrius, the husband he has chosen for her, because she is in love with another man, Lysander. Egeus asks permission from Theseus to invoke an old Athenian law and have Hermia put to death if she continues to disobey. Instead, Theseus offers Hermia the options of marrying Demetrius, being executed under the law, or being sent to a convent and spending the rest of her life as a nun. He gives her until the day of his and Hippolyta's wedding to decide what she wants to do. Hermia and Lysander, left alone, come up with a plan to meet in the woods the following night and run away to Lysander's aunt, who will give them a place to live outside Athens. Helena, who's in love with Demetrius, arrives, bemoaning the fact that Demetrius doesn't love her but loves Hermia instead. Hermia tells Helena that soon she won't have to worry about any rivalry between them, because she and Lysander are leaving town. Hermia gives Helena the details of their plan. Helena decides to tell Demetrius about it, hoping he'll appreciate her for helping him find Hermia.

Meanwhile, the Mechanicals are making plans to put on a play as entertainment for Theseus and Hippolyta's wedding. Quince, Bottom, Flute, Snout, Snug, and Starveling choose a romantic tragedy based on the story of Pyramus and Thisbe, but their utter lack of theatrical knowledge makes it clear that the play will be more comic than tragic. They, too, plan to meet in the woods the following night to rehearse their play.

Act 1, Scene 1

Athens, the palace of Theseus

[Enter **Theseus**, **Hippolyta**, **Philostrate**, and **Attendants**]

[Theseus, Hippolyta, Philostrate, and their Attendants enter the scene]

Athens: As you'll see, the setting of the play bears little resemblance to the Athens we know from ancient Greek literature, and Theseus's palace is very much like an English nobleman's country estate. But because Athens was revered as an ideal city in Shakespeare's time (the Renaissance developed in Europe partly through renewed appreciation for the Greek classics), Shakespeare may have set his play in Athens—the backdrop of so many mythological heroes and events—to show that the world of the play is a special one where magical things can happen.

Theseus and Hippolyta: Theseus, king of Athens, and Hippolyta, queen of the Amazons, are well-known figures of Greek mythology. Shakespeare based his version of these characters on the historian Plutarch's **Lives of the Noble Greeks and Romans**, also called **Parallel Lives** or **Plutarch's Lives**, written in the first century c.e.

THESEUS

1 Now, fair Hippolyta, our nuptial hour
Draws on apace; four happy days bring in
Another moon: but, O, methinks, how slow
This old moon wanes! she lingers my desires,
5 Like to a step-dame or a dowager
Long withering out a young man's revenue.

Now, beautiful Hippolyta, our wedding day is drawing near. In four days, on the new moon, we will marry. But, oh, this old moon is taking so long to fade away! It's keeping me from what I want, like a rich old widow hanging on and on and draining a young man's inheritance.

HIPPOLYTA

Four days will quickly steep themselves in night;
Four nights will quickly dream away the time;

And then the moon, like to a silver bow

10   New-bent in heaven, shall behold the night

Of our solemnities.

Four days will quickly turn to nights, and those four nights will quickly pass in dreams. And then the thin crescent of the moon, like a silver bow curved against the skies, will gaze down on our wedding ceremony.

THESEUS

Go, Philostrate,

Stir up the Athenian youth to merriments;

Awake the pert and nimble spirit of mirth;

15   Turn melancholy forth to funerals;

The pale companion is not for our pomp.

Go, Philostrate, and tell the young people of Athens to prepare for fun and celebration. Save the sorrow for funerals; we don't need any long faces at our celebration.

---

pale companion: In Shakespeare's day, paleness was considered a sign of sadness or melancholy, and "companion" could be a contemptuous term for someone who was bad company.

[Exit **Philostrate**]

*[**Philostrate** leaves the scene]*

Hippolyta, I woo'd thee with my sword,

And won thy love, doing thee injuries;

But I will wed thee in another key,

20   With pomp, with triumph and with revelling.

Hippolyta, I courted you with my sword, and won you by force. But I'll marry you a different way—with festivities, ceremonies, and celebration.

I woo'd thee with my sword: In Greek mythology, Theseus attacked the Amazons, a tribe of powerful female warriors, and kidnapped their queen, Hippolyta. The picture painted here is of a fierce woman now quiet and subdued as she submits to marriage with a stronger man. In Shakespeare's time, there was a great deal of anxiety about Queen Elizabeth I's refusal to marry. The English people worried that the queen would die without a successor and leave the country vulnerable to takeover by a foreign power. Some commentators have suggested that strong and independent Queen Hippolyta's willingness to marry Theseus is Shakespeare's personification of sixteenth-century English people's wishful thinking.

But I will wed thee in another key: Here, Theseus introduces one of the views of love found in the play—that love is a battle between the sexes. Although Theseus captured Hippolyta in battle, he sees their marriage as an opportunity for him to transform that brutal beginning into true and lasting love. As you'll see, other characters in the play will confront the same issue.

[Enter **Egeus, Hermia, Lysander,** and **Demetrius**]

*[**Egeus, Hermia, Lysander,** and **Demetrius** enter the scene]*

EGEUS

Happy be Theseus, our renowned duke!

Long live Theseus, our distinguished duke!

duke: In Shakespeare's time, this term was commonly used in connection with ancient Greek leaders. The word comes from Latin ***ducere***, meaning "to lead."

THESEUS

Thanks, good Egeus: what's the news with thee?

Thank you, good Egeus. What brings you here?

EGEUS

Full of vexation come I, with complaint
Against my child, my daughter Hermia.
25   Stand forth, Demetrius. My noble lord,
This man hath my consent to marry her.
Stand forth, Lysander: and my gracious duke,
This man hath bewitch'd the bosom of my child;
Thou, thou, Lysander, thou hast given her rhymes,
30   And interchanged love-tokens with my child:
Thou hast by moonlight at her window sung
With feigning voice verses of feigning love
And stolen the impression of her fantasy

With bracelets of thy hair, rings, gawds, conceits,
35 Knacks, trifles, nosegays, sweetmeats, messengers
Of strong prevailment in unharden'd youth:
With cunning hast thou filch'd my daughter's heart,
Turn'd her obedience, which is due to me,
To stubborn harshness: and, my gracious duke,
40 Be it so she will not here before your grace
Consent to marry with Demetrius,
I beg the ancient privilege of Athens,
As she is mine, I may dispose of her:
Which shall be either to this gentleman
45 Or to her death, according to our law
Immediately provided in that case.

I've come here, frustrated and angry, to register a complaint against my daughter, Hermia. Step forward, Demetrius. My noble lord, this man has my permission to marry Hermia. Step forward, Lysander. And here, my fine duke, is a man who has used magic to cast a spell on my daughter. You, you, Lysander, gave my daughter poems and exchanged gifts of love with her. On moonlit nights, you stood under her window and sang songs of phony love in a phony voice, and you made her fall in love with you. You captured her imagination with bracelets made from your hair, with rings and toys and cute little trinkets, knickknacks, trifles, flowers, and candy—all the signs and symbols of love that can turn a young girl's head. Your trickery stole my daughter's heart, and the obedience she owes me has turned to stubbornness. And, my gracious duke, if she should refuse to stand before you and agree to marry Demetrius, I ask you to grant me the privilege of ancient Athenian law, which allows me to do as I like with her, since she is my daughter. And that means either giving her to this gentleman or sending her straight to her death, which I will not hesitate to do if she continues to defy me.

---

bracelets of thy hair, rings: Locks of hair or bracelets made of hair were considered very serious tokens of romantic love. And note how precisely Egeus lists every item he thinks Lysander used to win over Hermia. Very specific lists like this one appear throughout the play.

As she is mine, I may dispose of her: For a comedy, this play certainly begins on a surprisingly grim note, as an angry father asks the local ruler for permission to kill his own daughter if she refuses to marry the man chosen for her. There are echoes here of *Romeo and Juliet*, in which Lord Capulet threatens to turn Juliet out into the streets if she does not consent to marry Paris. This scene also calls to mind a later play, **Othello**, in which Desdemona's father, Brabantio, claims that the Moorish general Othello won his daughter's heart with witchcraft.

THESEUS

What say you, Hermia? be advised, fair maid:
To you your father should be as a god;
One that composed your beauties, yea, and one
50   To whom you are but as a form in wax
By him imprinted and within his power
To leave the figure or disfigure it.
Demetrius is a worthy gentleman.

Well, Hermia, what do you have to say for yourself? Don't be rash, young lady—you should think of your father as a god. He's the one who gave you your beauty, and to him you're like a figure that he made from wax in his own image. He has the power to either leave that figure alone or leave it disfigured. Demetrius is a fine young man.

you are but as a form in wax: The image of a father as a god, and of his child as a wax figure, is related to creation stories from two traditions. According to Greek legend, Prometheus, a member of the powerful family of Titans who lived on Earth, fashioned small figures out of clay and then showed them to his powerful cousin Zeus, who breathed life into them, creating the human race. And in Genesis, a book of the Old Testament in the Christian Bible, God forms the first human being from clay and breathes life into him.

HERMIA

So is Lysander.

So is Lysander.

Hermia and her father are at war over her right to love the man she wants to love—another example of love as a battle.

THESEUS

55   In himself he is;
    But in this kind, wanting your father's voice,
    The other must be held the worthier.

Considered as an individual, yes, he is. But in this case, and in view of your father's wishes, Demetrius has to be seen as the better choice.

HERMIA

    I would my father look'd but with my eyes.

I wish my father could see him through my eyes.

THESEUS

    Rather your eyes must with his judgment look.

Well, you need to see this through his eyes instead.

HERMIA

60   I do entreat your grace to pardon me.
    I know not by what power I am made bold,
    Nor how it may concern my modesty,
    In such a presence here to plead my thoughts;
    But I beseech your grace that I may know
65   The worst that may befall me in this case,
    If I refuse to wed Demetrius.

Please pardon me, your grace. I don't know what makes me think I have the right to speak so directly to you, or whether pleading my case to a powerful lord like you will make me seem bold and immodest. But I beg your grace to tell me the worst thing that could happen to me if I refuse to marry Demetrius.

THESEUS

    Either to die the death or to abjure
    Forever the society of men.
    Therefore, fair Hermia, question your desires;
70   Know of your youth, examine well your blood,
    Whether, if you yield not to your father's choice,

You can endure the livery of a nun,
For aye to be in shady cloister mew'd,
To live a barren sister all your life,
75 Chanting faint hymns to the cold fruitless moon.
Thrice-blessed they that master so their blood,
To undergo such maiden pilgrimage;
But earthlier happy is the rose distill'd,
Than that which withering on the virgin thorn
80 Grows, lives and dies in single blessedness.

You can be put to death, or you can give up normal human society and the company of men for the rest of your life. So ask yourself what you really want, lovely Hermia. Consider how young you are, and examine your feelings closely. Do you really want to disobey your father and live the life of a nun, forever shut away in a dark convent, unmarried and childless, singing hymns to the cold, barren moon? There are some young women who have enough control over their passions to freely choose that path, and they will be blessed in Heaven. But here on Earth, the rose that is plucked and distilled into perfume is happier than the rose that withers on its untouched branch, growing, living, and dying in its unmarried holiness.

livery: This is a word meaning "uniform," and so it means the habit of a nun. Theseus is also saying that putting on the habit is not just a matter of adopting a certain mode of dress. It also means putting oneself under the visible sign of a life consigned to virginity.

the cold fruitless moon: The goddess of the moon—Diana, also known as Artemis—is also the goddess of virginity.

earthlier happy is the rose distill'd: Although the play is set in ancient Athens, it is marked by the religious traditions and beliefs of sixteenth-century England. Nuns, for example—childless virgins—were not seen favorably in Protestant England, because they were associated with Roman Catholicism. People in Shakespeare's England believed in a heavenly afterlife, but they also thought that having children was a route to earthly immortality. What Theseus is saying here is that a woman's essence passes into her children, just as the essence of a picked rose passes into perfume, but the rose that is never picked and remains on the branch will wither away and leave nothing of itself behind on Earth. This imagery involving roses is not surprising in a play that gives the natural world such a powerful role.

HERMIA

So will I grow, so live, so die, my lord,
Ere I will my virgin patent up
Unto his lordship, whose unwished yoke
My soul consents not to give sovereignty.

Then let me grow and live and die in just that way, my lord. I'd rather do that than give my virginity and my freedom to a man my soul rejects as its master.

THESEUS

85 Take time to pause; and, by the next new moon—
The sealing-day betwixt my love and me,
For everlasting bond of fellowship—
Upon that day either prepare to die
For disobedience to your father's will,
90 Or else to wed Demetrius, as he would;
Or on Diana's altar to protest
For aye austerity and single life.

Take some time to think, and by the next new moon—by the day of my marriage to my love—make up your mind to die for disobeying your father, to follow your father's order and marry Demetrius, or to throw yourself in protest onto Diana's altar and into an unmarried, barren life.

DEMETRIUS

Relent, sweet Hermia: and, Lysander, yield
Thy crazed title to my certain right.

Give in, sweet Hermia. And you, Lysander, surrender your worthless claim to what truly belongs to me.

LYSANDER

95 You have her father's love, Demetrius;
Let me have Hermia's: do you marry him.

You have her father's love, Demetrius. Let me have Hermia's. You can go ahead and marry him.

EGEUS

> Scornful Lysander! true, he hath my love,
> And what is mine my love shall render him.
> And she is mine, and all my right of her
> 100 I do estate unto Demetrius.

Aren't you clever, Lysander! But, yes, it's true—I do love Demetrius. And because I do, he can have everything that belongs to me. My daughter belongs to me, so it's my perfect right to give her to Demetrius.

LYSANDER

> I am, my lord, as well derived as he,
> As well possess'd; my love is more than his;
> My fortunes every way as fairly rank'd,
> If not with vantage, as Demetrius';
> 105 And, which is more than all these boasts can be,
> I am beloved of beauteous Hermia:
> Why should not I then prosecute my right?
> Demetrius, I'll avouch it to his head,
> Made love to Nedar's daughter, Helena,
> 110 And won her soul; and she, sweet lady, dotes,
> Devoutly dotes, dotes in idolatry,
> Upon this spotted and inconstant man.

I come from as good a family as he does, my lord, and I'm just as rich. I love her more than he does. In every way, I am equal to or better than Demetrius. And the most important thing is that Hermia loves me, so why shouldn't I insist on my right to marry her? Besides—and I'll swear this right to his face—Demetrius came on to Helena, Nedar's daughter, and got her to fall for him. And now that poor sweet girl idolizes this faithless, shady character.

---

dotes: To dote meant to love in a particularly foolish, hopeless way. The word is related to the word **dotage**, meaning old age, when people were thought to have lost the power to think clearly.

THESEUS

> I must confess that I have heard so much,
> And with Demetrius thought to have spoke thereof;
> 115 But, being over-full of self-affairs,
> My mind did lose it. But, Demetrius, come;
> And come, Egeus; you shall go with me,
> I have some private schooling for you both.
> For you, fair Hermia, look you arm yourself
> 120 To fit your fancies to your father's will;
> Or else the law of Athens yields you up—
> Which by no means we may extenuate—
> To death, or to a vow of single life.
> Come, my Hippolyta: what cheer, my love?
> 125 Demetrius and Egeus, go along:
> I must employ you in some business
> Against our nuptial and confer with you
> Of something nearly that concerns yourselves.

> *Yes, I must say, I had heard about that and thought I should have a talk with Demetrius, but I got caught up in my own affairs and forgot about it. Now, though, Demetrius and Egeus, come with me. I have some things I'd like to discuss privately with you. And as for you, lovely Hermia, you should find some way to want what your father wants—your marriage to Demetrius. Otherwise—and there won't be anything that anyone can do about it—you'll be bound by law either to die or commit yourself to a life with no marriage at all. Well, Hippolyta, my love, how are you doing? Come along. And please do come with us, Demetrius and Egeus. I need your help with some matters concerning our wedding, and I'd like to talk with you about something of importance to both of you.*

EGEUS

> With duty and desire we follow you.

> *It's our duty and our privilege to go with you.*

> [Exeunt all but **Lysander** and **Hermia**]
> *[Everyone but **Lysander** and **Hermia** leaves the scene]*

LYSANDER

130   How now, my love! why is your cheek so pale?
How chance the roses there do fade so fast?

Why so pale, my love? How did those roses in your cheeks fade so fast?

> This is typical of Lysander's teasing. He knows, of course, why Hermia looks so pale—she has just been given three terrible choices for her life—but he's trying to lighten the mood.

HERMIA

Belike for want of rain, which I could well
Beteem them from the tempest of my eyes.

Probably from lack of rain, which I could certainly give them with the storm of tears that's brewing in my eyes.

LYSANDER

Ay me! for aught that I could ever read,
135   Could ever hear by tale or history,
The course of true love never did run smooth;
But, either it was different in blood,—

Oh well! From everything I've ever heard, and in every story or history book I've ever read, true love has never taken an easy path. Either the lovers were from different social classes—

> **The course of true love never did run smooth:** This is one of the best-known lines from the play. It also sums up one of its major themes—that love is hard, and that crazy things can happen in the presence of true love. In the passages that follow, Lysander and Hermia continue to list all the things that can go wrong just by chance when something as random as love strikes.

HERMIA

O cross! too high to be enthrall'd to low.

Oh, how awful—being highborn and falling for someone from the lower orders.

LYSANDER

Or else misgraffed in respect of years,—

Or mismatched in age—

HERMIA

140   O spite! too old to be engaged to young.

That's terrible! So old that someone young is out of reach.

LYSANDER

Or else it stood upon the choice of friends,—

Or the choice was left up to others—

HERMIA

O hell! to choose love by another's eyes.

Oh, how hellish to have someone else make that choice for you!

LYSANDER

Or, if there were a sympathy in choice,
War, death, or sickness did lay siege to it,
145   Making it momentary as a sound,
Swift as a shadow, short as any dream;
Brief as the lightning in the collied night,
That, in a spleen, unfolds both heaven and earth,
And ere a man hath power to say "Behold!"
150   The jaws of darkness do devour it up:
So quick bright things come to confusion.

Or, if the choice was agreeable, then war, death, or sickness besieged it and made love transient as a passing sound, fleeting as a shadow, brief as a dream—the fitful flash of lightning in the black of night that tears open heaven and earth alike. And before a man can say, "Look!" it disappears into the jaws of darkness. That's how swiftly bright things come to ruin.

---

spleen: The spleen was thought to be the bodily origin of sudden impulses and passions. To say that lightning flashes "in a spleen" is to suggest its animation by an impulsive, passionate spirit—again, not a surprising image in a dramatic work where nature is also a character of sorts.

HERMIA

If then true lovers have been ever cross'd,
It stands as an edict in destiny:
Then let us teach our trial patience,
155 Because it is a customary cross,
As due to love as thoughts and dreams and sighs,
Wishes and tears, poor fancy's followers.

If true lovers have always been foiled, then being foiled must be their fate. So let's be patient with it. This is just a normal part of love, the same way thoughts, dreams, sighs, wishes, and tears follow the movements of the heart.

LYSANDER

A good persuasion: therefore, hear me, Hermia.
I have a widow aunt, a dowager
160 Of great revenue, and she hath no child:
From Athens is her house remov'd seven leagues;
And she respects me as her only son.
There, gentle Hermia, may I marry thee;
And to that place the sharp Athenian law
165 Cannot pursue us. If thou lovest me then,
Steal forth thy father's house to-morrow night;
And in the wood, a league without the town,
Where I did meet thee once with Helena,
To do observance to a morn of May,
170 There will I stay for thee.

I like that thinking. So listen, Hermia. I have an aunt, a widow, who has plenty of money but no children. She lives seven leagues from Athens and thinks of me as her only son. We can get married there, beyond the clutches of the harsh Athenian law. If you love me, sneak out of your father's house tomorrow night and meet me in those woods where I met you and Helena one morning in May, about a league outside of town. I'll wait for you there.

league: This is an old unit of measure, considered equal to the distance a man could walk in an hour. It probably was about three miles, and so seven leagues is roughly twenty-one miles.

HERMIA

> My good Lysander!
> I swear to thee, by Cupid's strongest bow,
> By his best arrow with the golden head,
> By the simplicity of Venus' doves,
> 175 By that which knitteth souls and prospers loves,
> And by that fire which burn'd the Carthage queen,
> When the false Troyan under sail was seen,
> By all the vows that ever men have broke,
> In number more than ever women spoke,
> 180 In that same place thou hast appointed me,
> To-morrow truly will I meet with thee.

My dear Lysander! I swear to you on Cupid's strongest bow, on his best golden-headed arrow, on the innocent doves of Venus, on everything that ties souls together and makes love grow, on the fire that burned Queen Dido when the unfaithful Aeneas sailed away, on all the vows ever broken by men, which outnumber all the vows ever spoken by women, that I'll meet you in the place you've chosen. Tomorrow I will absolutely meet you there.

Hermia's promise to Lysander takes the form of a list that grows progressively grimmer. She starts with happy images of love, such as that of Cupid and his golden arrow, and Venus and her innocent doves. But then she shifts to the depressing story of Dido and Aeneas, the protagonists of Virgil's **Aeneid**, in which Dido, the queen of Carthage, throws herself onto a funeral pyre when she is abandoned by Aeneas, a Trojan. Hermia then proceeds to swear on the number of vows broken by men, which outnumber the vows spoken by women. It's a dark list of love's dangers, and Hermia recites it with comic unknowing. Note the contrast between the increasingly somber imagery and the lightness of the four sets of rhyming couplets, beginning with "By the simplicity of Venus' doves." (A rhyming couplet is a unit of two lines whose final words rhyme, as in "queen / seen" and "broke / spoke.")

LYSANDER

Keep promise, love. Look, here comes Helena.

Keep your promise, my love. Look—here comes Helena.

[Enter **Helena**]
*[**Helena** enters the scene]*

HERMIA

God speed fair Helena! whither away?

Good day, beautiful Helena! Where are you going?

God speed: This expression evolved from "God speed you on your way," which was originally a blessing and a wish for good luck on a venture. "God speed" later became as common a greeting as "good morning" or "how are you?"

HELENA

Call you me fair? that fair again unsay.
185 Demetrius loves your fair: O happy fair!
Your eyes are lode-stars; and your tongue's sweet air
More tuneable than lark to shepherd's ear,
When wheat is green, when hawthorn buds appear.
Sickness is catching: O, were favour so,
190 Yours would I catch, fair Hermia, ere I go;
My ear should catch your voice, my eye your eye,
My tongue should catch your tongue's sweet melody.
Were the world mine, Demetrius being bated,
The rest I'd give to be to you translated.
195 O, teach me how you look, and with what art
You sway the motion of Demetrius' heart.

Did you just call me beautiful? Then take it back! It's your beauty that Demetrius loves. And such a lucky beauty—eyes like guiding stars, a voice that sounds more beautiful than the lark's song does to a shepherd in the spring, when the wheat is green and the hawthorns are budding. Sickness is contagious, so I wish I could catch your beauty, too, Hermia. My ear would sicken with your voice, my eye would be infected by your eye, my tongue would be laid low by your tongue's musical speech. If I owned the world and everything in it, I'd give it all up—everything but Demetrius—to become you. Oh, teach me how to look like you, and show me what you did to win his heart.

Helena's speech (again, note the sets of rhyming couplets) outlines another of the play's major themes—transformation. Helena begins by wishing that she could come down with a case of Hermia's beauty, with all the "favors," or features, that made Demetrius fall in love with her friend, and she finishes with a declaration of what she would give to be "translated," or turned, into Hermia.

HERMIA

I frown upon him, yet he loves me still.

I frown at him, but he loves me anyway.

HELENA

O that your frowns would teach my smiles such skill!

Oh, if only your frowns could teach my smiles how to have that effect!

HERMIA

I give him curses, yet he gives me love.

He gets curses from me but gives me love.

HELENA

200 O that my prayers could such affection move!

Oh, if only my prayers could make him feel that kind of affection for me!

HERMIA

The more I hate, the more he follows me.

The more I hate him, the more he follows me around.

HELENA

> The more I love, the more he hateth me.
>
> *The more I love him, the more he hates me.*

HERMIA

> His folly, Helena, is no fault of mine.
>
> *He's a fool, Helena, but that's not my fault.*

HELENA

> None, but your beauty: would that fault were mine!
>
> *No, it's your beauty's fault. And that's one fault I'd like to have!*

HERMIA

> 205   Take comfort: he no more shall see my face;
> Lysander and myself will fly this place.
> Before the time I did Lysander see,
> Seem'd Athens as a paradise to me:
> O, then, what graces in my love do dwell,
> 210   That he hath turn'd a heaven unto a hell!
>
> *Be happy. He won't see my face anymore. Lysander and I are leaving this place. Before I saw Lysander, Athens was like a paradise to me. Oh, what is it about this love that has turned this heaven into a hell!*

LYSANDER

> Helen, to you our minds we will unfold:
> To-morrow night, when Phoebe doth behold
> Her silver visage in the watery glass,
> Decking with liquid pearl the bladed grass,
> 215   A time that lovers' flights doth still conceal,
> Through Athens' gates have we devised to steal.
>
> *Helena, we'll tell you our secret plan. Tomorrow night, when the moon sees her reflection in the water and adorns the blades of grass with pearls of light—a time that always gives cover to fleeing lovers—we plan to steal away through the gates of Athens.*

Phoebe: This is the name of the moon. In Greek mythology, Phoebe is the sister of Phoebus, god of the sun.

HERMIA

And in the wood, where often you and I
Upon faint primrose-beds were wont to lie,
Emptying our bosoms of their counsel sweet,
220 There my Lysander and myself shall meet;
And thence from Athens turn away our eyes,
To seek new friends and stranger companies.
Farewell, sweet playfellow: pray thou for us;
And good luck grant thee thy Demetrius!
225 Keep word, Lysander: we must starve our sight
From lovers' food till morrow deep midnight.

In the woods where you and I often went to lie on beds of pale primroses, telling each other sweet secrets, Lysander and I will meet and then turn our eyes away from Athens, to find new friends and the company of strangers. Farewell, sweet friend of my childhood. Pray for us, and may luck bring your Demetrius to you. Keep your promise, Lysander. We must deprive ourselves of the sight of each other until tomorrow, way past midnight.

LYSANDER

I will, my Hermia.

I will, dear Hermia!

[Exit **Hermia**]
*[**Hermia** leaves the scene]*

Helena, adieu:
As you on him, Demetrius dote on you!

Good-bye, Helena—may Demetrius cherish you as you do him!

[Exit]
*[**Lysander** leaves the scene]*

HELENA

230 How happy some o'er other some can be!
Through Athens I am thought as fair as she.
But what of that? Demetrius thinks not so;
He will not know what all but he do know:
And as he errs, doting on Hermia's eyes,
235 So I, admiring of his qualities:
Things base and vile, folding no quantity,
Love can transpose to form and dignity:
Love looks not with the eyes, but with the mind;
And therefore is wing'd Cupid painted blind:
240 Nor hath Love's mind of any judgement taste;
Wings and no eyes figure unheedy haste:
And therefore is Love said to be a child,
Because in choice he is so oft beguiled.
As waggish boys in game themselves forswear,
245 So the boy Love is perjured every where:
For ere Demetrius look'd on Hermia's eyne,
He hail'd down oaths that he was only mine;
And when this hail some heat from Hermia felt,
So he dissolved, and showers of oaths did melt.
250 I will go tell him of fair Hermia's flight:
Then to the wood will he to-morrow night
Pursue her; and for this intelligence
If I have thanks, it is a dear expense:
But herein mean I to enrich my pain,
255 To have his sight thither and back again.

How strange that some people can be so much happier than others. Throughout Athens, people think I am as pretty as Hermia, but what does that matter? Demetrius doesn't think so. He will not see what everyone else can see. And just as he mistakenly fawns over Hermia's eyes, so do I marvel at his qualities, which are low and repellent. Love can take things that are ugly and deformed and give them a beautiful shape and dignity. Love doesn't come from the eyes, but from the mind; that's why Cupid is always painted with a blindfold on. The mind of Love has no judgment or taste; and with wings but without sight, of course Love will be careless and hasty. That's why Love is depicted as a child, because his choices so often seem like childish mistakes. In the same way that boys tell lies for fun, the boy god

Love is often lied to. Before Demetrius looked into Hermia's eyes, he showered me with promises, saying that he was mine alone. But when this icy hail of promises felt some heat from Hermia, he and his promises melted away. I will tell him about Hermia's plans so that he will go to the woods tomorrow night to follow her. If he thanks me for giving him this information, it will be worth the pain of seeing him chase after her. But that pain will be lessened by giving me the chance to see him go and come back again.

So the boy Love is perjured every where: This passage expresses one of Shakespeare's big ideas about love—it doesn't make sense, and it plays tricks on the one who loves. This idea is embodied by the image of Cupid, the blindfolded god of love, who shoots his arrows randomly, making the wrong people fall in love with each other. The notion that love is blind, and that the mind, not the eyes, is what falls in love, may seem to suggest that it doesn't matter whether the object of love is good-looking or not. But what Helena actually means is that love can make the lover blind to the loved one's bad qualities, or it can make someone fall for the wrong person—besides playing tricks, love makes mistakes.

If I have thanks, it is a dear expense: After speaking at length about the tricks that love can play, Helena comes up with a plan that is at worst mean (telling on her friend just to win favor with the man she loves) and at best astonishingly self-defeating. Helena hopes that Demetrius will suddenly fall back in love with her after he sees that he has to give up on Hermia. And here is another of the play's love-related themes—love makes people do stupid things.

Act 1 of the play has dealt exclusively with the first of the three groups of characters we will meet—the Athenians. Shakespeare uses the characters' speech patterns to define each of the groups. The noble Athenians generally speak in **iambic pentameter** (pronounced "eye-AM-bic pen-TA-muh-ter"), also known as **blank verse**, which is common in English poetry, just as it is in ordinary spoken English. This verse form gets the first part of its name from its **foot**, which is the term for the particular syllabic unit that is repeated to form a line of iambic pentameter—in this case, the foot is an **iamb**, or a pair of syllables in which the first syllable is unstressed and the second is stressed (a stressed syllable is one that is emphasized when it's spoken). The second part of the verse form's name comes from its **meter**, which is the term for the number of feet in a line of this type of verse. In this case, we know that we're dealing with **pentameter** because there are five iambs in every line (you probably remember that the prefix **penta** has to do with the number five). So, in a nutshell, a line of verse written in iambic pentameter is a line in which there are five pairs of iambs. Here's an example from Helena's speech (words all in caps are stressed):

and THEREfore IS love SAID to BE a CHILD,
beCAUSE in CHOICE he IS so OFT beGUILED

And, as we've seen before, the young lovers' long speeches often include sets of rhyming couplets.

[Exit]
[*Helena* leaves the scene]

Act 1, Scene 2

Athens, Quince's house

[Enter **Quince, Snug, Bottom, Flute, Snout**, and **Starveling**]

[Quince, Snug, Bottom, Flute, Snout, and Starveling enter the scene]

These characters, tradesmen of Athens, are known as the Mechanicals, after Puck's labeling of them as "rude mechanicals" (act 3, scene 2). Puck's description is based on his assumptions about people who work with their hands.

QUINCE

1 Is all our company here?

Is everyone here?

The Mechanicals' last names are related to their work. Quince is related to the word **quoins** or **quines**, a wedge of wood used by a carpenter.

BOTTOM

You were best to call them generally, man by man,
according to the scrip.

It would be best if you were to call the name of each man in general, as seen on the list.

Bottom, the weaver's name, comes from the bottom, or core, that was used to wind thread. He is overconfident, pompous, and prone to verbal mix-ups when he tries to use big words. Here he uses "generally" when he means "individually."

QUINCE

Here is the scroll of every man's name, which is
5 thought fit, through all Athens, to play in our
interlude before the duke and the duchess, on his
wedding-day at night.

Here is the list of everyone, from all of Athens, who we think is fit to be in the play that we'll perform for the duke and duchess on the night of their wedding day.

BOTTOM

First, good Peter Quince, say what the play treats
on, then read the names of the actors, and so grow
10   to a point.

First, Peter Quince, tell us what the play is about, and then tell us who will play which part, and come to the end.

QUINCE

Marry, our play is, The most lamentable comedy, and
most cruel death of Pyramus and Thisby.

Indeed, our play is The Terribly Sad Comedy and Most Horrible Death of Pyramus and Thisby.

The name of the play's Babylonian protagonist is spelled Thisbe, but Shakespeare's script spells her name Thisby whenever it is spoken by one of the Mechanicals or appears in their script. Here, we'll follow Shakespeare's spelling of her name when it comes to the Mechanicals' dialogue and the text of their play, but otherwise her name will be spelled Thisbe. (Shakespeare may have been using the variant spelling Thisby to underscore the tradesmen's relative ignorance of the theater and of classical literature.)

most lamentable comedy: This combination of words shows us that the Mechanicals don't know what they're doing. The play they have chosen is based on a real story—it appears in Ovid's **Metamorphoses**—but it's actually a tragedy about two young lovers who are kept apart by their families and can communicate only through the wall that separates them. They plan to run away together, but after a series of mistakes they both end up dead. The story is considered one of the sources for **Romeo and Juliet**, which Shakespeare also wrote around this time.

BOTTOM

A very good piece of work, I assure you, and a
merry. Now, good Peter Quince, call forth your
15   actors by the scroll. Masters, spread yourselves.

This is an excellent play, I tell you, and very funny. Now, good Peter Quince, call out your actors from that list. Line up, men.

QUINCE

Answer as I call you. Nick Bottom, the weaver.

Answer when I call your name. Nick Bottom, the weaver.

BOTTOM

Ready. Name what part I am for, and proceed.

Ready. Tell me what part I play, and then go on.

QUINCE

You, Nick Bottom, are set down for Pyramus.

You, Nick Bottom, will play Pyramus.

BOTTOM

What is Pyramus? a lover, or a tyrant?

Who is Pyramus? A lover, or a fierce and terrible king?

QUINCE

20   A lover, that kills himself most gallant for love.

A lover who kills himself most nobly for love.

BOTTOM

That will ask some tears in the true performing of
it: if I do it, let the audience look to their
eyes; I will move storms, I will condole in some
measure. To the rest: yet my chief humour is for a
25   tyrant: I could play Ercles rarely, or a part to
tear a cat in, to make all split.

The raging rocks
And shivering shocks

Shall break the locks
30 Of prison gates;
And Phibbus' car
Shall shine from far
And make and mar
The foolish Fates.

35 This was lofty! Now name the rest of the players.
This is Ercles' vein, a tyrant's vein; a lover is
more condoling.

I'll need to cry to make my performance seem real. And if I do, the members of the audience will cry their own eyes out from all my weeping. I will cause storms of tears, and speak so mournfully. Go on, name the others—actually, what I really want is to play a tyrant. I could play Hercules like no one else, or a part that needs a lot of ranting and create a great riot. Listen.

The raging rocks
And shivering shocks
Shall break the locks
Of prison gates;
And Phibbus' car
Shall shine from far
And make and mar
The foolish Fates.

Wasn't that amazing? All right, tell us the rest of the actors. But first let me say that what I just did was in the style of Hercules, the tyrant. Of course a lover would have to tug on the audience's heartstrings.

Ercles: Bottom is referring here to ***Hercules Furens*** (***The Madness of Hercules***), a play by Lucius Annaeus Seneca, or Seneca the Younger, usually just called Seneca, a Roman poet who lived from 4 B.C.E. to 65 C.E. The part of Hercules calls for a lot of ranting and raving.

Phibbus' car: Bottom is referring to Phoebus, god of the sun, and his chariot. Phoebus was believed to ride across the sky from morning until night, pulling the sun behind him.

Now name the rest of the players: Bottom repeatedly tells Quince to continue but is so self-absorbed that he can't help making himself the focus again and again.

QUINCE

Francis Flute, the bellows-mender.

Francis Flute, the bellows repairer.

A bellows is an instrument filled with air. When the bellows is squeezed, the air inside is directed outward through a small nozzle in a thin stream. Bellows have been used by metalworkers and blacksmiths, and a pipe organ also includes a bellows as one of its components.

FLUTE

Here, Peter Quince.

I'm here, Peter Quince.

QUINCE

40   Flute, you must take Thisby on you.

Flute, you will play Thisby.

FLUTE

What is Thisby? a wandering knight?

Who is Thisby? A knight on a mission?

---

a wandering knight: When Flute hears Thisbe's name, he imagines the kind of knight errant who figured in the great romantic poems of the day—someone brave, handsome, and chivalrous, wandering the countryside and seeking adventure.

QUINCE

It is the lady that Pyramus must love.

She is the lady Pyramus loves.

FLUTE

Nay, faith, let me not play a woman; I have a beard coming.

No! Please don't make me play a woman. I'm in the middle of growing a beard.

Women weren't allowed onstage in Shakespeare's time, and so young boys played female roles. Here, Flute gets a double dose of humiliation as he's told not only to play a woman but also to play a part usually taken by a teenage boy.

QUINCE

That's all one: you shall play it in a mask, and
45   you may speak as small as you will.

That's all right. You'll be wearing a mask, and you can speak in a tiny high voice.

BOTTOM

An I may hide my face, let me play Thisby too, I'll
speak in a monstrous little voice. "Thisne,
Thisne"; "Ah, Pyramus, lover dear! thy Thisby dear,
and lady dear!"

*Oh, if I can hide my face, then I can play Thisby, too! I'll speak in a terribly high little voice. [**Bottom** speaks in a deep voice] "Thisne, Thisne." [**Bottom** speaks in a high-pitched voice] "Ah, Pyramus, my dear lover! It's your dear Thisby, your dear lady!"*

QUINCE

50   No, no; you must play Pyramus: and, Flute, you Thisby.

No, no. You have to just play Pyramus. Flute, you have to play Thisby.

BOTTOM

Well, proceed.

All right, go on.

QUINCE

Robin Starveling, the tailor.

Robin Starveling, the tailor.

The tailor's name, Starveling, is also a noun or an adjective that denotes or describes someone who is quite thin, as if from starvation. According to some commentators, the prevailing Elizabethan stereotype of tailors was that they were very lean, and this notion led to the proverb "Nine tailors make a man" (for example, see the website of the Chicago Shakespeare Theater on Navy Pier, http://www.chicagoshakes.com/main.taf?p=2,62,7,1,7). That stereotype may account for Starveling's name, but this view of the proverb's origins is far from unanimous.

STARVELING

Here, Peter Quince.

I'm here, Peter Quince.

QUINCE

Robin Starveling, you must play Thisby's mother.
55   Tom Snout, the tinker.

Robin Starveling, you must play Thisby's mother. Tom Snout, the tinker.

A tinker sold things like pots and pans. Snout's name is a play on the word spout, the "nose" of a teakettle.

SNOUT

Here, Peter Quince.

I'm here, Peter Quince.

QUINCE

You, Pyramus' father: myself, Thisby's father:
Snug, the joiner; you, the lion's part: and, I
hope, here is a play fitted.

You will play Pyramus's father, and I will play Thisby's father. Snug the Joiner, you will play the lion—and that, I hope, is a cast for a play.

A joiner makes fine furniture, and so Snug's name appears to be complimentary, since all the elements of a well-made piece of furniture should fit tightly together.

SNUG

60   Have you the lion's part written? pray you, if it
be, give it me, for I am slow of study.

Do you have the lion's part written out yet? If you do, please give it to me, because I learn slowly.

QUINCE

You may do it extempore, for it is nothing but roaring.

You can just make it up as you go along, because all you do is roar.

---

extempore: This word means "extemporaneously," that is, without preparation or rehearsal. It comes from the Latin preposition **ex** (which can mean "free of") and from **tempore**, the objective case of the noun **tempus** (meaning "time").

BOTTOM

Let me play the lion, too: I will roar, that I will
do any man's heart good to hear me; I will roar,
65   that I will make the duke say "Let him roar again,
let him roar again."

Let me play the lion, too. I will roar so loud that it will impress any man who hears me. I will roar so brilliantly that the duke will say, "Let him roar again, let him roar again."

QUINCE

An you should do it too terribly, you would fright
the duchess and the ladies, that they would shriek;
and that were enough to hang us all.

If you roar too loudly and horribly, you'll frighten the duchess and the ladies, and they'll scream. Then they'll hang us all.

ALL

70   That would hang us, every mother's son.

That would make them hang us, every one of us.

BOTTOM

    I grant you, friends, if that you should fright the
    ladies out of their wits, they would have no more
    discretion but to hang us: but I will aggravate my
    voice so that I will roar you as gently as any
75   sucking dove; I will roar you an 'twere any
    nightingale.

I know, friends, that if you should frighten the ladies that much, then they'll have to hang us. But I will aggravate my voice to roar as softly as a sweet little dove. I will make a roar that sounds like a nightingale.

---

aggravate: Bottom mixes up his words again. What he really means is not that he will "aggravate" his voice (that is, irritate it or make it angry) but that he will moderate or soften it.

QUINCE

    You can play no part but Pyramus; for Pyramus is a
    sweet-faced man; a proper man, as one shall see in a
    summer's day; a most lovely gentleman-like man:
80   therefore you must needs play Pyramus.

You can play no other part but Pyramus, because Pyramus is a handsome man, as perfect a man as you'll see on a summer's day, a most gentlemanly man. Therefore, you must play Pyramus.

Quince tries to control Bottom with flattery.

BOTTOM

Well, I will undertake it. What beard were I best
to play it in?

Well, I'll do it, then. What kind of beard would look best for this part?

QUINCE

Why, what you will.

Why, whatever you want.

BOTTOM

I will discharge it in either your straw-colour
85   beard, your orange-tawny beard, your purple-in-grain
beard, or your French-crown-colour beard, your
perfect yellow.

*I will perform it in either a light yellow beard, or a light orange-brown beard, or a
dyed-purple beard, or a bright yellow beard the color of a French crown.*

A French crown was a coin, and so Bottom means a shade of gold like the color
of the coin.

QUINCE

Some of your French crowns have no hair at all, and
then you will play bare-faced. But, masters, here
90   are your parts: and I am to entreat you, request
you and desire you, to con them by to-morrow night;
and meet me in the palace wood, a mile without the
town, by moonlight; there will we rehearse, for if
we meet in the city, we shall be dogged with
95   company, and our devices known. In the meantime I
will draw a bill of properties, such as our play
wants. I pray you, fail me not.

*Well, some of those French heads have no hair at all, so then you'd have to play
it beardless. But, gentlemen, here are your scripts, and I beg you, plead with you,
and demand of you to learn them by heart by tomorrow night. Then meet me in the*

woods by the palace, about a mile outside the town, by moonlight. We'll rehearse there—if we met in the city, we'd be bothered by others, and our plans would be discovered. In the meantime, I will draw up a list of props that we'll need in the play. I ask you not to fail me.

French crowns have no hair at all: This is a pun based on the notion of hair loss as an indication of syphilis, a sexually transmitted disease often called "the French disease."

meet me in the palace wood: Like Hermia and Lysander, the Mechanicals plan to meet in the forest. In this way, the plot moves the play's mortal characters out of the civilized city and into a place where strange and wild things can happen.

BOTTOM

We will meet; and there we may rehearse most
obscenely and courageously. Take pains; be perfect: adieu.

We will meet there and rehearse most vulgarly and bravely. Work hard and be perfect with your lines. Good-bye.

---

obscenely: This is another mix-up from Bottom. He may be focusing on the "scene" portion of *obscenely* to give the word a meaning ("dramatic") that is somewhat appropriate to the theater, or he may be confusing *scene* with *seen* and trying to create a word that means "unseen." Or he may just mean *seemly*, that is, in a manner appropriate to the occasion. Given the frequent ambiguity of Bottom's language, there is room for interpretation when it comes to how his character should be played in any particular production of *A Midsummer Night's Dream*.

QUINCE

100   At the duke's oak we meet.

Then we'll meet at the duke's oak.

BOTTOM

Enough; hold or cut bow-strings.

Enough. Everyone, stick to the plan, or we're done for.

Just like the noble Athenians, the Mechanicals have their own way of speaking. Since they're plain working folk, Shakespeare has them speak in straight prose.

[Exeunt]

[Everyone leaves the scene]

Act 2

Act 2 Summary

Act 1 ended with Hermia and Lysander planning to meet in the woods, and with Helena intending to tell Demetrius about their plan. The Mechanicals were also making plans to meet in the woods the same night to rehearse their play.

Act 2 introduces the play's third group of characters, the fairies, whose attempt to solve their own problems gets them mixed up in those of the Athenians and the Mechanicals. Oberon and Titania, king and queen of the fairies, have been arguing over a changeling boy that Titania has in her custody. Oberon wants the boy as his page, or servant, but Titania refuses to give him up. Meanwhile, their conflict has been throwing the weather and the world into chaos, but Titania, who is attached to the boy because his deceased mother was a good friend of hers, still won't relent. Oberon summons Puck, his jester and henchman, and tells him to look for a flower that he knows has been shot with an arrow by Cupid, the god of love. If juice from this flower is placed on a sleeping person's eyes, that person will fall madly, foolishly in love with the first person or thing he or she sees upon waking up. Oberon wants to play a prank on Titania by using the flower's juice to make her fall in love with someone disgusting. He hopes that in exchange for freeing her from that spell, she'll relinquish the boy. Puck dashes off to get the flower. While waiting for Puck to return, Oberon sees Helena chasing after Demetrius, who insults her cruelly and threatens to harm her if she won't leave him alone. Puck comes back, and Oberon, out of pity for Helena, tells Puck to take some of the love juice from the flower and put it on the eyes of Demetrius so that he will fall in love with her, but he describes Demetrius only as a young Athenian. When Titania falls asleep in another part of the woods, Oberon sneaks up on her, dabs her eyes with the love juice, and disappears.

Lysander and Hermia, exhausted, arrive in the woods and decide it's time to rest. Hermia tells Lysander to find a place to sleep some distance from her, but Lysander says that he should sleep next to her. He insists that he won't try anything improper, but Hermia holds her ground, and Lysander finds a spot apart from her. Puck arrives and, mistaking Lysander for Demetrius, puts the love juice on Lysander's eyes. Helena wanders into the clearing just as Lysander is waking up. Lysander sees her and falls madly in love with her. Helena can't believe Lysander's vows of love, and she thinks he's making fun of her. She runs off, with Lysander chasing after her. Hermia wakes up alone and frightened, and she sets off to find Lysander.

Act 2, Scene 1

A forest near Athens

[Enter a **Fairy** at one door, and **Puck** at another]

*[A **Fairy** enters at one door, and **Puck** enters at another]*

PUCK

1   How now, spirit! whither wander you?

Hello, spirit! Where are you going?

FAIRY

Over hill, over dale,
Thorough bush, thorough brier,
Over park, over pale,
5   Thorough flood, thorough fire,
I do wander every where,
Swifter than the moon's sphere;
And I serve the Fairy Queen,
To dew her orbs upon the green.
10   The cowslips tall her pensioners be;
In their gold coats spots you see;
Those be rubies, fairy favours,
In those freckles live their savours.
I must go seek some dewdrops here,
15   And hang a pearl in every cowslip's ear.
Farewell, thou lob of spirits; I'll be gone.
Our Queen and all her elves come here anon.

Over the hills and valleys, through the bushes and thorny patches, over parks and enclosed spaces, through flood, through fire, I wander everywhere, more quickly than the moon turns around the earth in its orbit. I serve the Fairy Queen, sprinkling dew on her fairy circles on the green grass. The cowslips standing tall are her bodyguards, wearing coats of gold covered in dots, which are rubies, love gifts from the fairies. Those dots are where their sweet perfume comes from. Now I must find some dewdrops and hang a pearl on the ear of every cowslip. Farewell, you rough, dumb spirit. I must go. The Queen and all her elves will be here soon.

In Shakespeare's day, fairies were already a long-accepted element of country folklore, denizens of the pre-Christian magical world of nature. They were thought to be mischievous creatures who wreaked havoc when people weren't looking. If something went wrong without an explanation, people could blame it on the fairies, elves, or spirits. When Christianity came along, people weren't quite ready to give up the idea of fairies, so they decided that fairies were fallen angels, trapped on Earth, who caused trouble because they were amoral.

pale: This was an enclosure of land. You may be familiar with the phrase "beyond the pale," used in connection with actions that most people would consider to be out of bounds.

moon's sphere: In the classical era in which the play is set, people believed that Earth was the center of the universe, and that heavenly bodies, such as the moon, traveled around our planet in transparent spheres.

orbs: This word refers to fairy rings, or circles in a meadow where rings of grass seem lighter than the rest of the grass. Such rings were believed to have been made by fairies.

pensioners: The queen's royal bodyguards were called her "gentleman pensioners."

lob: This word refers to a country bumpkin—a silly, dense person.

PUCK

The King doth keep his revels here to-night;
Take heed the Queen come not within his sight;
20   For Oberon is passing fell and wrath,
Because that she as her attendant hath
A lovely boy, stolen from an Indian king.
She never had so sweet a changeling;
And jealous Oberon would have the child
25   Knight of his train, to trace the forests wild;
But she perforce withholds the loved boy,
Crowns him with flowers, and makes him all her joy.
And now they never meet in grove or green,
By fountain clear, or spangled starlight sheen,

30 But they do square, that all their elves for fear
Creep into acorn cups and hide them there.

The king is having his party here tonight. Make sure the queen doesn't come
anywhere near him because Oberon is really angry at her. One of her attendants is
a beautiful boy, taken from an Indian king, and she's never had such a wonderful
stolen child. Now Oberon is jealous and wants the boy to be his page and lead his
servants through the wild forest. But she holds on to the boy with all her might, put-
ting crowns of flowers on his head and making him her beloved. Now the king and
queen never meet in the forest or meadow, near a clear fountain, or under starlight
without fighting so terribly that all their elves, terrified, crawl into their acorn cups
and hide themselves there.

---

changeling: In folklore, fairies and elves sometimes kidnap mortal children, leaving elf or fairy children in their place. The word **changeling** can mean either the
fairy child or the mortal child who is now living in the wrong world.

square: This verb means "to quarrel." Oberon and Titania, like Egeus and Hermia, and like Theseus and Hippolyta in the past, are another warring pair.

FAIRY

Either I mistake your shape and making quite,
Or else you are that shrewd and knavish sprite
Call'd Robin Goodfellow. Are not you he
35 That frights the maidens of the villagery,
Skim milk, and sometimes labour in the quern,
And bootless make the breathless housewife churn,
And sometime make the drink to bear no barm,
Mislead night-wanderers, laughing at their harm?
40 Those that Hobgoblin call you, and sweet Puck,
You do their work, and they shall have good luck.
Are not you he?

Unless I'm mistaken, you have the form of that clever and mischievous spirit known
as Robin Goodfellow. Aren't you the one who frightens the village maids, skims the
cream off the milk, messes around with the grain mill, makes the housewife churn
and churn her milk without it turning to butter, who makes the beer go flat, and
makes people lose their way at night, then laughs at their trouble? Some call you

Hobgoblin and sweet Puck; you do their work for them and bring good luck. Are you not he?

Robin Goodfellow: This is the name of a male fairy common in country folklore. As this passage shows, he was blamed for all manner of things that went awry. Shakespeare, having grown up in a country town, would have been very familiar with this figure.

quern: This is a mill for grinding grain.

bootless: This word means "futilely" or "to no avail."

PUCK

> Thou speakest aright:
> I am that merry wanderer of the night.
> 45   I jest to Oberon, and make him smile
> When I a fat and bean-fed horse beguile,
> Neighing in likeness of a filly foal;
> And sometime lurk I in a gossip's bowl
> In very likeness of a roasted crab,
> 50   And, when she drinks, against her lips I bob,
> And on her withered dewlap pour the ale.
> The wisest aunt, telling the saddest tale,
> Sometime for three-foot stool mistaketh me;
> Then slip I from her bum, down topples she,
> 55   And "tailor" cries, and falls into a cough;
> And then the whole quire hold their hips and laugh,
> And waxen in their mirth, and neeze, and swear
> A merrier hour was never wasted there.
> But room, fairy, here comes Oberon.

You are right. I am that fun-loving one who wanders in the night, making jokes and playing tricks to make Oberon laugh. When I see a fat old horse, I trick him by neighing as if I were a pretty young filly. Sometimes I hide in the bottom of an old woman's cup, disguised as a roasted crab apple. Then, when she lifts it up to drink, I bounce against her lips and make her spill the beer all over her wrinkled old neck. Sometimes the wisest old woman, with a serious story to tell, will mistake me for a three-legged stool. When she tries to sit on me, I slide from under her butt, and down she goes, crying out as she falls on her ass and coughs. Then the whole company laughs hard, holding on to their hips and bending over until they cough and sneeze, swearing that they've never had such a good time. But make room, fairy! Here comes Oberon.

And "tailor" cries: Tailors sat on the ground, or on benches, with their legs crossed as they worked. The old woman cries "tailor" because she falls into that position.

FAIRY

60   And here my mistress. Would that he were gone!

And here's my lady. Oh, if only he weren't here!

[Enter **Oberon** at one door, with his **Train**, and **Titania**, at another, with hers]
*[**Oberon** enters at one door with his **Attendants**, and **Titania** enters at another with her **Attendants**]*

OBERON

Ill met by moonlight, proud Titania.

We meet unhappily under the moon, proud Titania.

TITANIA

What, jealous Oberon! Fairies, skip hence;
I have forsworn his bed and company.

Oh look, it's jealous Oberon. Let's go, fairies. I have sworn to stay out of his bed and will not speak with him.

Here we have still another warring pair, trying to turn conflict into (or back into) love.

OBERON

Tarry, rash wanton; am not I thy lord?

Hold on, you hasty tramp. Am I not your husband?

TITANIA

65 Then I must be thy lady; but I know
When thou hast stolen away from fairy land,
And in the shape of Corin sat all day,
Playing on pipes of corn, and versing love
To amorous Phillida. Why art thou here,
70 Come from the farthest steep of India,
But that, forsooth, the bouncing Amazon,
Your buskin'd mistress and your warrior love,
To Theseus must be wedded, and you come
To give their bed joy and prosperity?

Then I guess I must be your wife. But I know that you have sneaked out of fairyland and spent days disguised as a country boy, playing on a corn pipe and flirting with a lovelorn country girl. Why did you come here from the far mountains of India? It must have been to see that Amazon, your boot-wearing mistress and your warrior lover, who now is about to marry Theseus. I suppose you've come to offer them congratulations on their marriage.

Corin and Phillida: These were common names for the young shepherds and shepherdesses, or country boys and girls, found in pastoral poetry, which celebrates life in the country.

the bouncing Amazon: Titania insinuates that Oberon and Hippolyta, the Amazon queen now engaged to Theseus, were lovers. In many productions of *A Midsummer Night's Dream*, the actors who play Theseus and Hippolyta also play Oberon and Titania, suggesting that the wild fairies are an alternate, magical version of the calm, steady Theseus and Hippolyta seen at the opening of the play.

OBERON

75 How canst thou thus, for shame, Titania,
Glance at my credit with Hippolyta,
Knowing I know thy love to Theseus?
Didst not thou lead him through the glimmering night
From Perigouna, whom he ravished?
80 And make him with fair Aegles break his faith,
With Ariadne and Antiopa?

How can you shamelessly try to hurt my good name by accusing me of being with Hippolyta, especially when I know that you loved Theseus? Weren't you the one who led Theseus away from Perigouna after he raped her? Then made him unfaithful to Aegles, Ariadne, and Antiopa?

According to Plutarch's biography, Theseus met, loved, and abandoned many women while out on his adventures. Perigouna was the daughter of the brigand Sinis, whom the young Theseus killed while traveling to Athens the first time. Aegles was a nymph. Ariadne was the daughter of Minos, king of the island of Crete. She helped Theseus kill the Minotaur in exchange for him helping her to escape from Crete, but on the way back to Athens, Theseus abandoned her on another island. In some stories, Antiopa is another name for Hippolyta, whereas in other stories she is a different Amazon queen, perhaps Hippolyta's sister.

TITANIA

    These are the forgeries of jealousy;
    And never, since the middle summer's spring,
    Met we on hill, in dale, forest, or mead,
85 By paved fountain, or by rushy brook,
    Or in the beached margent of the sea,
    To dance our ringlets to the whistling wind,
    But with thy brawls thou hast disturb'd our sport.
    Therefore the winds, piping to us in vain,
90 As in revenge, have suck'd up from the sea
    Contagious fogs; which, falling in the land,
    Hath every pelting river made so proud
    That they have overborne their continents.
    The ox hath therefore stretch'd his yoke in vain,
95 The ploughman lost his sweat, and the green corn
    Hath rotted ere his youth attain'd a beard;
    The fold stands empty in the drowned field,
    And crows are fatted with the murrion flock;
    The nine men's morris is fill'd up with mud,
100 And the quaint mazes in the wanton green,
    For lack of tread, are undistinguishable.
    The human mortals want their winter here;
    No night is now with hymn or carol blest;

Therefore the moon, the governess of floods,
105 Pale in her anger, washes all the air,
That rheumatic diseases do abound.
And thorough this distemperature we see
The seasons alter: hoary-headed frosts
Fall in the fresh lap of the crimson rose;
110 And on old Hiems' thin and icy crown
An odorous chaplet of sweet summer buds
Is, as in mockery, set. The spring, the summer,
The childing autumn, angry winter, change
Their wonted liveries; and the mazed world,
115 By their increase, now knows not which is which.
And this same progeny of evils comes
From our debate, from our dissension;
We are their parents and original.

These are lies that come from your jealousy. Since the beginning of midsummer, my fairies and I have not been able to meet on a hill, in a valley, in a forest or a meadow, by a pebbled spring or brook edged with rushes, or by the shore of the sea to do our ritual dances in the whistling wind without being interrupted by you and your noisy fighting. Then, since we can't dance for them, the winds, in revenge, have sucked nasty fogs up from the sea, which fall on the land and make all the little rivers so proud that they have overflowed their banks. Then the fields are flooded and the green corn is drowned, and all the hard work of the oxen pulling their yokes, and of the ploughman, has been for nothing. The sheep pens are empty, and the crows feast on the bodies of sheep dead from disease. The game squares are filled with mud, and the mazes made by the boys in the thick green grass can't be found, because no one has walked through them and left a path. The mortal humans want their winter now. They haven't had any nights for hymns or blessed carols. So the moon, which governs floods, pale and angry, washes the air so that all the diseases of cold wet weather come down and attack everyone. And throughout this disturbance in the natural order, we see the seasons altered: white-headed frosts land on young red roses; a crown of fragrant summer flowers is set on the head of Hiems, god of winter, as if to make fun of him. The spring, the summer, the fruitful autumn, angry winter, have all changed their usual clothes, and the world, confused by what the seasons produce, does not know which is which. These evil products come from our quarrel, our fight. We are their parents and responsible for their origin.

they have overborne their continents: Titania is saying that their fighting has caused the rivers to overflow their banks and flood the land. Some commentators believe that Shakespeare may have been making a reference to a series of bad harvests that were due to poor weather and that led to food shortages in the 1590s.

nine men's morris: This was a game that used a set of squares marked out in the dirt.

the quaint mazes . . . are indistinguishable: The mazes are outlined in the grass, but with no one walking over the grass, the paths cannot be seen.

human mortals want their winter here: Some editions of the play give this phrase as *winter cheer*. Both phrases mean essentially the same thing—it has not seemed like winter, and so people have not been able to enjoy the usual winter festivities, with their hymns and carols.

the moon, the governess of floods: Renaissance-era people understood that the moon and the tides were related, and so the moon is described here as responsible for flooding. But people of the time did not understand that diseases are passed by way of germs, and so they believed that "rheumatic diseases," such as colds and flu, came from bad, cold, damp air.

this same progeny of evils: Titania is saying that the whole natural world has been thrown into disorder because she and Oberon have been quarreling.

OBERON

> Do you amend it, then; it lies in you.
> 120 Why should Titania cross her Oberon?
> I do but beg a little changeling boy
> To be my henchman.

You can put an end to it. That's in your power. Why should Titania argue with her Oberon? All I'm asking is for your little changeling boy to become my page.

TITANIA

> Set your heart at rest;
> The fairy land buys not the child of me.
> 125 His mother was a vot'ress of my order;
> And, in the spiced Indian air, by night,

Full often hath she gossip'd by my side;
And sat with me on Neptune's yellow sands,
Marking th' embarked traders on the flood;
130 When we have laugh'd to see the sails conceive,
And grow big-bellied with the wanton wind;
Which she, with pretty and with swimming gait
Following—her womb then rich with my young squire—
Would imitate, and sail upon the land,
135 To fetch me trifles, and return again,
As from a voyage, rich with merchandise.
But she, being mortal, of that boy did die;
And for her sake do I rear up her boy;
And for her sake I will not part with him.

Don't even think about it. I wouldn't give that child up for the entire fairy world. His mother was devoted to my order. We would often sit together at night on the beach in the exotic Indian air, gossiping and watching the traders' ships sailing on the flood tide. We laughed to see the ships' sails full and round with wind, as if the wind had made them pregnant. Then she, pregnant with my young changeling, with a belly as round as the sails, would imitate them and sail along the land to fetch me gifts, returning again with the merchandise, just as the ships did from their voyages. But she was a mortal, and she died in childbirth. For her sake, I am bringing up her boy, and for her sake, I will not give him up.

---

vot'ress: A votaress or votary is a worshipper in a cult or a religion.

OBERON

140 How long within this wood intend you stay?

How long do you plan to stay here in these woods?

TITANIA

Perchance till after Theseus' wedding-day.
If you will patiently dance in our round,
And see our moonlight revels, go with us;
If not, shun me, and I will spare your haunts.

Probably until after Theseus's wedding day. If you want to dance our circle dance with us and take part in our moonlight celebrations, then you can come with us. If not, leave me alone, and I will stay out of your usual places.

OBERON

145   Give me that boy and I will go with thee.

Give me the boy, and I will go with you.

TITANIA

Not for thy fairy kingdom. Fairies, away!
We shall chide downright if I longer stay.

Not for your fairy kingdom. Let's go, fairies! We will start fighting if I stay any longer.

[Exit **Titania** with her **Train**]
[Titania leaves the scene with her Attendants]

OBERON

Well, go thy way; thou shalt not from this grove
Till I torment thee for this injury.
150   My gentle Puck, come hither. Thou rememb'rest
Since once I sat upon a promontory,
And heard a mermaid on a dolphin's back
Uttering such dulcet and harmonious breath
That the rude sea grew civil at her song,
155   And certain stars shot madly from their spheres
To hear the sea-maid's music.

Well, go on your way. I won't let you leave this forest until I've made you pay for this insult. My good Puck, come here. Do you remember how I once sat upon a cliff and heard a mermaid on a dolphin's back singing such a beautiful song that the rough sea grew calm and stars shot through the sky to come and hear the mermaid sing?

PUCK

I remember.

I remember.

OBERON

That very time I saw, but thou couldst not,
Flying between the cold moon and the earth
160   Cupid, all arm'd; a certain aim he took
At a fair vestal, throned by the west,
And loos'd his love-shaft smartly from his bow,
As it should pierce a hundred thousand hearts;
But I might see young Cupid's fiery shaft
165   Quench'd in the chaste beams of the wat'ry moon;
And the imperial vot'ress passed on,
In maiden meditation, fancy-free.
Yet mark'd I where the bolt of Cupid fell.
It fell upon a little western flower,
170   Before milk-white, now purple with love's wound,
And maidens call it Love-in-idleness.
Fetch me that flow'r, the herb I showed thee once.
The juice of it on sleeping eye-lids laid
Will make or man or woman madly dote
175   Upon the next live creature that it sees.
Fetch me this herb, and be thou here again
Ere the leviathan can swim a league.

You couldn't see this, but that same night, I saw Cupid flying between the moon and the earth. He took aim at a vestal virgin, who sat on a throne in the west, and shot his love arrow so strongly from his bow that it seemed as if it could pierce a hundred thousand hearts. But Cupid's flaming arrow was put out by the watery beams of the virginal moon, and the royal worshipper went on, still maidenly and fancy free. Yet I saw where Cupid's arrow fell, upon a small western flower that once was white as milk but now was purple from the wounds of love. Maidens call it "Love in idleness." Go and get me that flower, the one I once showed you. When the juice from that flower is placed on the eyelids of someone who is asleep, it will make that person, whether a man or a woman, fall madly in love with the first living creature he or she sees. Get me that flower, and come back here before a whale can swim a league.

a fair vestal, throned by the west: A vestal virgin was a woman dedicated to a religious order who had vowed to remain a virgin. "Throned by the west" is probably a reference to Queen Elizabeth I. The idea is that Cupid tried to make her fall in love, but he failed, and she remained pure and virginal. This passage is believed to be a compliment to the queen, possibly invoking imagery from a water pageant, or a parade on a river, that the Earl of Hertford staged for the queen in 1591.

Love-in-idleness: Oberon is describing a pansy.

PUCK

> I'll put a girdle round about the earth
> In forty minutes.

I'll fly around the world in forty minutes.

This was an era of dramatic world exploration and expansion. In 1580, Sir Francis Drake completed his voyage around the world—only the second such adventure in history—and the world suddenly seemed much smaller to the Elizabethans.

[Exit **Puck**]
*[**Puck** leaves the scene]*

OBERON

180   Having once this juice,
> I'll watch Titania when she is asleep,
> And drop the liquor of it in her eyes;
> The next thing then she waking looks upon,
> Be it on lion, bear, or wolf, or bull,

185   On meddling monkey, or on busy ape,
> She shall pursue it with the soul of love.
> And ere I take this charm from off her sight,
> As I can take it with another herb,
> I'll make her render up her page to me.

190   But who comes here? I am invisible;
> And I will overhear their conference.

Once I have that juice, I'll watch Titania, and when she falls asleep, I'll put a drop of it on each of her eyes. When she wakes up, she'll chase after the first thing she sees, whether it's a lion, a bear, a wolf or a bull, a mischievous monkey, or a busy ape. And before I lift that spell from her eyes (as I can do with another flower), I'll make her give her page to me. But who goes there? I am invisible, so I will listen to what they say.

I am invisible: Oberon needs to make it clear to the audience that he, a fairy, can't be seen by the Athenians.

[Enter **Demetrius**, **Helena** following him]
*[**Demetrius** enters the scene, with **Helena** right behind him]*

DEMETRIUS

> I love thee not, therefore pursue me not.
> Where is Lysander and fair Hermia?
> The one I'll slay, the other slayeth me.
> 195   Thou told'st me they were stol'n unto this wood,
> And here am I, and wood within this wood,
> Because I cannot meet my Hermia.
> Hence, get thee gone, and follow me no more.

I don't love you, so don't follow me. Where are Lysander and beautiful Hermia? I'll kill Lysander; Hermia's killing me. You told me they were hiding in these woods, and here I am, like a madman, because I cannot find my Hermia. Go on, go away. Don't follow me anymore.

---

wood within this wood: In some editions of the play, the word **wood**, meaning "insane," is given as **wode**, although the word is pronounced the same as "wood."

HELENA

> You draw me, you hard-hearted adamant;
> 200   But yet you draw not iron, for my heart
> Is true as steel. Leave you your power to draw,
> And I shall have no power to follow you.

You draw me to you, you magnet. But you're not attracting dull iron, because my heart is as faithful as fine steel. Lose your power to attract me, and I'll have no power to follow you.

DEMETRIUS

Do I entice you? Do I speak you fair?
Or, rather, do I not in plainest truth
205   Tell you I do not nor I cannot love you?

*Do I lead you on? Do I sweet-talk you? Or do I tell you as clearly as I can that I do
not and cannot love you?*

HELENA

And even for that do I love you the more.
I am your spaniel; and, Demetrius,
The more you beat me, I will fawn on you.
Use me but as your spaniel, spurn me, strike me,
210   Neglect me, lose me; only give me leave,
Unworthy as I am, to follow you.
What worser place can I beg in your love,
And yet a place of high respect with me,
Than to be used as you use your dog?

*And because you say that, I love you even more. I am your spaniel, Demetrius, and
the more you beat me, the more I will worship you. Treat me like your spaniel—
ignore me, hit me, neglect me, lose me. Just let me follow you, unworthy though I am
to be loved by you. What lower place in your heart could there be than the place of a
dog, though that's a place I value highly?*

A major theme in the play is that love is uncontrollable and makes people do
crazy or foolish things. Here, Helena shows that she is willing to humiliate herself and do foolish things just for the sake of being near Demetrius.

DEMETRIUS

215   Tempt not too much the hatred of my spirit;
For I am sick when I do look on thee.

*Don't make me hate you even more than I already do, because it makes me sick to
look at you.*

HELENA

And I am sick when I look not on you.

And it makes me sick not to look at you.

DEMETRIUS

You do impeach your modesty too much
To leave the city and commit yourself
220 Into the hands of one that loves you not;
To trust the opportunity of night,
And the ill counsel of a desert place,
With the rich worth of your virginity.

You're risking your reputation for modesty by leaving the city and putting yourself
into the hands of someone who doesn't love you. Being out at night in a deserted
area is a danger to your precious virginity.

At the time when this play was written, an unmarried girl who wasn't a virgin was
considered practically worthless.

HELENA

Your virtue is my privilege for that:
225 It is not night when I do see your face,
Therefore I think I am not in the night;
Nor doth this wood lack worlds of company,
For you, in my respect, are all the world.
Then how can it be said I am alone
230 When all the world is here to look on me?

Your excellence in my eyes is enough reason for me to take this risk. When I look
at you, I don't see the night, so I don't think I'm out in the night. These woods don't
seem lonely to me, because you are all the world to me. So how can it be said that I
am alone, when the whole world can see me here?

DEMETRIUS

I'll run from thee and hide me in the brakes,
And leave thee to the mercy of wild beasts.

I'll run from you and hide in the bracken ferns, leaving you to the mercy of
the wild beasts.

HELENA

The wildest hath not such a heart as you.
Run when you will; the story shall be chang'd:
235 Apollo flies, and Daphne holds the chase;
The dove pursues the griffin; the mild hind
Makes speed to catch the tiger; bootless speed,
When cowardice pursues and valour flies.

The wildest beast isn't as heartless as you. Run where you want. The story will be
different this time. Apollo will be chased by Daphne. The dove pursues the griffin;
the gentle deer chases after the tiger. Speed doesn't matter when the coward is the
hunter and the brave one is the prey.

In Greek mythology, the god Apollo chased after the nymph Daphne, planning
to rape her. She prayed for help and was saved when she was turned into
a laurel tree. Helena says that the story will be reversed, and that she will
chase Demetrius.

griffin: A griffin is powerful mythological creature. The majestic predator is said
to have the body, tail, and back legs of a lion and the heads and wings of an
eagle. Thought to have been the king of creatures, they are known for guarding
treasures and possessions.

DEMETRIUS

I will not stay thy questions; let me go;
240 Or, if thou follow me, do not believe
But I shall do thee mischief in the wood.

I won't listen to this anymore. Let me go. Or if you follow me, be forewarned that I
will do you wrong in these woods.

HELENA

Ay, in the temple, in the town, the field,
You do me mischief. Fie, Demetrius!
Your wrongs do set a scandal on my sex.

245 We cannot fight for love as men may do;
We should be woo'd, and were not made to woo.

Yes, you've done me wrong in the temple, in the town, in the field. Shame, Demetrius! You wrong all women. We aren't allowed to fight for love the way men do. We were made for lovers to court us, and were not made to do the courting ourselves.

[Exit **Demetrius**]
*[**Demetrius** leaves the scene]*

I'll follow thee, and make a Heaven of Hell,
To die upon the hand I love so well.

I'll follow you, and dying at the hand of the one I love so much will make a heaven of this hell.

[Exit **Helena**]
*[**Helena** leaves the scene]*

OBERON

Fare thee well, nymph; ere he do leave this grove,
250 Thou shalt fly him, and he shall seek thy love.

Good-bye, nymph. Before he leaves this forest, you will run from him, and he will seek your love.

[Re-enter **Puck**]
*[**Puck** reenters the scene]*

Hast thou the flower there? Welcome, wanderer.

Do you have the flower there? Welcome back, wanderer.

PUCK

Ay, there it is.

Yes, here it is.

OBERON

I pray thee give it me.
I know a bank where the wild thyme blows,
255 Where oxlips and the nodding violet grows,

Quite over-canopied with luscious woodbine,
With sweet musk-roses, and with eglantine;
There sleeps Titania sometime of the night,
Lull'd in these flowers with dances and delight;
260 And there the snake throws her enamell'd skin,
Weed wide enough to wrap a fairy in;
And with the juice of this I'll streak her eyes,
And make her full of hateful fantasies.
Take thou some of it, and seek through this grove:
265 A sweet Athenian lady is in love
With a disdainful youth; anoint his eyes;
But do it when the next thing he espies
May be the lady. Thou shalt know the man
By the Athenian garments he hath on.
270 Effect it with some care, that he may prove
More fond on her than she upon her love.
And look thou meet me ere the first cock crow.

*Please give it to me. [**Oberon** takes the flower from **Puck**] I know a riverbank where wild thyme, oxlips, and violets are growing, with a canopy of honeysuckle, sweet musk roses, and sweetbrier. Sometimes at night Titania sleeps there, lulled by the dancing, delightful flowers. There snakes shed their skin in pieces wide enough to make a fairy's bed. I'll streak her eyes with the juice of this flower, filling her with disgusting fantasies and desires. [**Oberon** gives part of the flower to **Puck**] Take some of the juice, and look through the forest. A beautiful Athenian girl is in love with a young man who has no interest in her. Put the juice on his eyes, but do it only when the next thing he sees will be this lady. You will know the man by the Athenian clothes he wears. Do this carefully, so he will be more in love with her than she is with him. Meet me back here before the first rooster crows in the morning.*

PUCK

Fear not, my lord; your servant shall do so.

Don't worry, master, I'll do it.

[Exeunt]
*[**Oberon** and **Puck** leave the scene]*

Act 2, Scene 2

Another part of the forest

[Enter **Titania**, with her train of **Fairies**]
*[**Titania** enters the scene with her following of **Fairies**]*

TITANIA

1   Come, now a roundel and a fairy song;
     Then, for the third part of a minute, hence;
     Some to kill cankers in the musk-rose buds,
     Some war with rere-mice for their leathern wings,
5   To make my small elves coats, and some keep back
     The clamorous owl that nightly hoots and wonders
     At our quaint spirits. Sing me now asleep;
     Then to your offices and let me rest.

Come now, dance in a circle, and sing a fairy song. And after that, some of you go to kill cankerworms in the musk rose buds, and some of you go fight the bats for their leather wings, so we can use them to make coats for my little elves. And some of you keep the noisy owl away, the one that hoots every night and stares at our pretty spirits. Sing me to sleep now, and then off to your assignments, and let me rest.

FIRST FAIRY

     [Singing] You spotted snakes with double tongue,
10   Thorny hedgehogs, be not seen;
     Newts and blind-worms, do no wrong,
     Come not near our fairy queen.

*[The **First Fairy** sings] You spotted snakes with your forked tongues, and you spiked hedgehogs—don't let yourselves be seen. Newts and blindworms, do no harm. Stay away from our fairy queen.*

Newts and blind-worms: Newts (or water lizards), blindworms, and spiders were believed to be poisonous.

FAIRIES

[Singing] Philomel, with melody
Sing in our sweet lullaby;
15 Lulla, lulla, lullaby, lulla, lulla, lullaby:
Never harm,
Nor spell nor charm,
Come our lovely lady nigh;
So, good night, with lullaby.

*[The other **Fairies** sing] Philomel, with your melody, sing our sweet lullaby. Let no harm, spells, or charms come near our lovely lady. Lullaby and good night.*

Philomel: In Ovid's work, Philomela, the daughter of King Pandion, is turned into a nightingale after being raped by Tereus, her brother-in-law.

FIRST FAIRY

20 [Singing] Weaving spiders, come not here;
Hence, you long-legg'd spinners, hence!
Beetles black, approach not near;
Worm nor snail, do no offence.

*[The **First Fairy** sings] You spiders weaving your webs, don't come around. Go away, spiders, go away. Stay back, black beetles. Worms and snails, don't cause trouble.*

Several of Shakespeare's plays include lyrics that are meant to be sung, but no particular music is specified, and so directors have to come up with their own music or turn to past productions. Many of Shakespeare's plays have been made into operas or had their song lyrics set to music by professional composers. The most famous example is probably Felix Mendelssohn's 1842 setting of this fairy song.

SECOND FAIRY

Hence, away! now all is well:
25 One aloof stand sentinel.

Go away! Now everything's fine. One of you, stand nearby to keep watch.

[Exeunt **Fairies**. **Titania** sleeps.]

*[All the **Fairies** leave the scene; **Titania** falls asleep]*

[Enter **Oberon** and squeezes the flower on Titania's eyelids]

*[**Oberon** enters the scene and squeezes the flower onto **Titania**'s eyelids]*

OBERON

> What thou seest when thou dost wake,
> Do it for thy true-love take,
> Love and languish for his sake:
> Be it ounce, or cat, or bear,
> 30 Pard, or boar with bristled hair,
> In thy eye that shall appear
> When thou wakest, it is thy dear:
> Wake when some vile thing is near.

Take for your true love the first thing you see when you awake. Love him and long for him. Whether he's a lynx, a cat, a bear, a leopard, or a bristle-haired boar, in your eyes he will seem like your dearest love. Wake up when some horrible thing comes near you.

[Exit]

*[**Oberon** leaves the scene]*

[Enter **Lysander** and **Hermia**]

*[**Lysander** and **Hermia** enter the scene]*

LYSANDER

> Fair love, you faint with wandering in the wood;
> 35 And to speak troth, I have forgot our way:
> We'll rest us, Hermia, if you think it good,
> And tarry for the comfort of the day.

Beautiful lover, you're exhausted from wandering in the woods. And, to tell the truth, I have lost the way. We'll rest here, Hermia, if you think it's a good idea, and wait until daylight, when it is easier to travel.

HERMIA

> Be it so, Lysander: find you out a bed;
> For I upon this bank will rest my head.

That's fine, Lysander. Go find a place to sleep. I'll rest right here on this bank.

LYSANDER

40 > One turf shall serve as pillow for us both;
> One heart, one bed, two bosoms and one troth.

This spot is fine for both of us. One heart, one bed, two bosoms, and one promise.

---

two bosoms and one troth: The word *bosom*, in this context, means the seat of love and intimate attachment. You've probably heard the expression "bosom friends," and the word should be understood in that sense here. A *troth* is a promise or pledge of faithfulness. The word figures in the adjective *betrothed*, which describes people who have exchanged a promise to marry, and it's related to the Old English word for truth.

HERMIA

> Nay, good Lysander; for my sake, my dear,
> Lie further off yet, do not lie so near.

No, dear Lysander. For my sake, please lie farther away. Don't sleep so close to me.

LYSANDER

> O, take the sense, sweet, of my innocence!
45 > Love takes the meaning in love's conference.
> I mean, that my heart unto yours is knit
> So that but one heart we can make of it;
> Two bosoms interchained with an oath;
> So then two bosoms and a single troth.
50 > Then by your side no bed-room me deny;
> For lying so, Hermia, I do not lie.

Oh, believe me, my intentions are innocent! Lovers should be able to understand each other. I just meant that my heart is bound to yours, and so it's as if we shared one heart. Our bosoms are linked by our promises to each other, and so there are two bosoms and one promise. Don't deny me. I want to lie with you, but that doesn't mean I'm lying to you.

---

lying so, Hermia, I do not lie: In the sixteenth century, to lie with someone often meant having sex with that person. Here, Lysander protests that he is not lying, or telling an untruth, when he says he actually just wants to lie next to Hermia. It's clear, though, that he actually has something else in mind (and Hermia knows it). Note that Demetrius has already told Helena that it's a bad idea for a virginal girl to go off in the woods at night with a man she shouldn't trust, but now it's Hermia who's in trouble with a man she thought she could trust.

HERMIA

Lysander riddles very prettily:
Now much beshrew my manners and my pride,
If Hermia meant to say Lysander lied.
55 But, gentle friend, for love and courtesy
Lie further off; in human modesty,
Such separation as may well be said
Becomes a virtuous bachelor and a maid,
So far be distant; and, good night, sweet friend:
60 Thy love ne'er alter till thy sweet life end!

Lysander, you speak very cleverly. A curse on me for even suggesting that you were lying. But, dear friend, for the sake of love and appearances, sleep somewhere away from me. It's only proper that a respectable boy and girl who aren't married should sleep separately. So stay away, and good night, sweet friend. May your love for me be this strong until your life ends.

LYSANDER

Amen, amen, to that fair prayer, say I;
And then end life when I end loyalty!
Here is my bed: sleep give thee all his rest!

Amen to that, I agree. And let my life end when I'm no longer loyal to you! Here's my bed. Sleep well!

Hermia wins this battle—Lysander backs off.

HERMIA

With half that wish the wisher's eyes be press'd!

May half of all the sleep you wish for me be yours!

[They sleep]
*[**Lysander** and **Hermia** fall asleep]*

[Enter **Puck**]
*[**Puck** enters the scene]*

PUCK

65 Through the forest have I gone.
But Athenian found I none,
On whose eyes I might approve
This flower's force in stirring love.
Night and silence. —Who is here?
70 Weeds of Athens he doth wear:
This is he, my master said,
Despised the Athenian maid;
And here the maiden, sleeping sound,
On the dank and dirty ground.
75 Pretty soul! she durst not lie
Near this lack-love, this kill-courtesy.
Churl, upon thy eyes I throw
All the power this charm doth owe.
When thou wakest, let love forbid
80 Sleep his seat on thy eyelid:
So awake when I am gone;
For I must now to Oberon.

*I've looked all through the forest and haven't found any Athenian upon whose eyes
I can place this juice that will cause love. It's dark and quiet. But wait—who's that?
He wears Athenian clothes. This must be the one my master told me about, the one
who hates that Athenian girl. And look, here's the girl, sleeping soundly on this damp,
dirty ground. Poor girl, she doesn't dare sleep near this creep. You jerk, I'm putting
all this love juice's power right on your eyes. When you wake up, may love keep you
from going back to sleep. So wake up when I'm gone. Now I'm off to find Oberon.*

In this passage, Puck speaks in a type of poetry that Shakespeare reserves for the fairies. This type of poetry is called **catalectic trochaic tetrameter**. Let's break that down. A **trochee** is a poetic foot in which one stressed syllable is followed by an unstressed syllable: **RA-ven**. (Recall that iambic pentameter uses a poetic foot consisting of one unstressed syllable followed by a stressed syllable: **a-WAY**.) Since the prefix **tetra** has to do with the number four, it stands to reason that trochaic tetrameter must be a line of verse consisting of four pairs of trochees. As for the term **catalectic**, it's an adjective describing a line of trochaic tetrameter in which the last syllable—what would have been the eighth of the line's eight syllables—is missing. So this means that a line of catalectic trochaic tetrameter has only three and a half trochees—seven syllables—rather than eight. Here's an example adapted from Puck's speech: **THROUGH the FORest HAS he GONE ()**, with the empty parentheses representing the missing eighth syllable. And that's the fairies' special way of speaking.

[Exit]

*[**Puck** leaves the scene]*

[Enter **Demetrius** and **Helena**, running]

*[**Demetrius** and **Helena** enter the scene, running]*

HELENA

Stay, though thou kill me, sweet Demetrius.

I want you to stop, sweet Demetrius, even if that means you'll kill me.

DEMETRIUS

I charge thee, hence, and do not haunt me thus.

I'm telling you, go away and don't follow me.

HELENA

85   O, wilt thou darkling leave me? do not so.

Are you going to leave me in the dark? Please don't.

DEMETRIUS

Stay, on thy peril: I alone will go.

If you stay here, you'll be taking your chances. I'm going on ahead, and I'm going alone.

[Exit]
*[**Demetrius** leaves the scene]*

HELENA

O, I am out of breath in this fond chase!
The more my prayer, the lesser is my grace.
Happy is Hermia, wheresoe'er she lies;
90   For she hath blessed and attractive eyes.
How came her eyes so bright? Not with salt tears:
If so, my eyes are oftener wash'd than hers.
No, no, I am as ugly as a bear;
For beasts that meet me run away for fear:
95   Therefore no marvel though Demetrius
Do, as a monster fly my presence thus.
What wicked and dissembling glass of mine
Made me compare with Hermia's sphery eyne?
*[sees **Lysander**]* But who is here? Lysander! on the ground!
100   Dead? or asleep? I see no blood, no wound.
Lysander if you live, good sir, awake.

*Oh, I am breathless from this foolish chase. The more I pray, the less I get. Hermia must be so happy, wherever she sleeps tonight, because she has such beautiful eyes. How did her eyes get so bright? Not from tears. If tears were the cause, my eyes have been washed in more tears than hers have. No, no, I am as ugly as a bear. Even animals that see me run away in terror from my looks. It's no wonder, then, that Demetrius runs from me as if he's seen a monster. What mean, lying mirror made me think I could compete with Hermia's starry eyes? [she sees **Lysander**] But who's that? Lysander! Lying on the ground! Is he dead? Or asleep? I don't see any blood or any wound. Lysander, if you're alive, wake up!*

LYSANDER

[waking] And run through fire I will for thy sweet sake.
Transparent Helena! Nature shows art,
That through thy bosom makes me see thy heart.
105 Where is Demetrius? O, how fit a word
Is that vile name to perish on my sword!

[waking up] I'd even run through fire for you if you asked. Bright Helena! Nature has a magic that lets me see into your heart. Where is Demetrius? Oh, my sword should put an end to that despicable name!

Here, Lysander means that he sees into Helena's heart and understands how much she loves Demetrius.

HELENA

Do not say so, Lysander; say not so
What though he love your Hermia? Lord, what though?
Yet Hermia still loves you: then be content.

Don't say that Lysander, don't say that just because he loves your Hermia. Lord, why should that matter? Hermia loves you, so be happy with that.

LYSANDER

110 Content with Hermia! No; I do repent
The tedious minutes I with her have spent.
Not Hermia but Helena I love:
Who will not change a raven for a dove?
The will of man is by his reason sway'd;
115 And reason says you are the worthier maid.
Things growing are not ripe until their season
So I, being young, till now ripe not to reason;
And touching now the point of human skill,
Reason becomes the marshal to my will
120 And leads me to your eyes, where I o'erlook
Love's stories written in love's richest book.

Happy with Hermia? No, I'm sorry for every boring minute I have ever spent with her. I don't love Hermia; I love Helena. Who wouldn't trade a raven for a dove? A man's desires can be swayed by his mind, and my mind says you are the better girl. Things do not ripen until the time is right. Until now, I was too young to think right. Now, though, I've gained enough understanding for reason to take over and lead me to your eyes, in which I see all of love's stories written in love's most beautiful book.

Lysander falls in love with Helena because of magic, and this highlights the theme of love as unreasonable and uncontrollable. Shakespeare is saying that it might as well be magic that causes people to fall in love, since love often makes little sense.

HELENA

Wherefore was I to this keen mockery born?
When at your hands did I deserve this scorn?
Is't not enough, is't not enough, young man,
125   That I did never, no, nor never can,
Deserve a sweet look from Demetrius' eye,
But you must flout my insufficiency?
Good troth, you do me wrong, good sooth, you do,
In such disdainful manner me to woo.
130   But fare you well: perforce I must confess
I thought you lord of more true gentleness.
O, that a lady, of one man refused,
Should of another therefore be abused!

Why was I born to be teased? What did I ever do to you that you now make fun of me? Isn't it enough that I can't get a kind look from Demetrius, but now you have to point out everything that's wrong with me? The truth is, it's wrong for you to pretend to love me in such a mean way. Good-bye. I must admit, I thought you were a nicer guy. Oh, how terrible that a girl who's been turned down by one man should then be treated so badly by another.

[Exit]
*[**Helena** leaves the scene]*

LYSANDER

She sees not Hermia. Hermia, sleep thou there:
135   And never mayst thou come Lysander near!
For as a surfeit of the sweetest things

> The deepest loathing to the stomach brings,
> Or as the heresies that men do leave
> Are hated most of those they did deceive,
140 So thou, my surfeit and my heresy,
> Of all be hated, but the most of me!
> And, all my powers, address your love and might
> To honour Helen and to be her knight!

She didn't see Hermia. Hermia, keep sleeping right there, and never come near me again! In the same way that eating too many sweets can make you sick to your stomach, or people who have given up a bad habit go on to hate that habit more than anyone else does, I hate you most of all, my bad old habit. I'll do everything in my power to honor Helena and be her hero.

[Exit]
*[**Lysander** leaves the scene]*

[**Hermia** wakes up]
*[**Hermia** wakes up]*

HERMIA

> [waking] Help me, Lysander, help me! Do thy best
145 To pluck this crawling serpent from my breast!
> Ay me, for pity! what a dream was here!
> Lysander, look how I do quake with fear:
> Methought a serpent eat my heart away,
> And you sat smiling at his cruel prey.
150 Lysander! what, removed? Lysander! lord!
> What, out of hearing? gone? no sound, no word?
> Alack, where are you speak, an if you hear;
> Speak, of all loves! I swoon almost with fear.
> No? then I well perceive you all not nigh
155 Either death or you I'll find immediately.

[waking up] Help me, Lysander, help me! Do everything you can to pull this snake off my chest! Oh my! What a horrible dream! Lysander, look at how I'm shaking. I dreamed that a snake was eating my heart away, and you sat there smiling as he attacked. Lysander! What, are you gone? Lysander! What, can't you hear me? No sound or word from you? For pity's sake, if you can hear me, speak up. Speak up,

for the sake of all true love! I'm almost fainting from fear. No? Then you must not be anywhere nearby. I'll find you, or I'll find death right away.

Snakes are an ancient symbol of untrustworthiness. Hermia's dream, in which Lysander does nothing while a snake destroys her heart, foreshadows what will happen to Hermia's emotions when she discovers that Lysander is now in love with Helena and hates her. The snake Hermia dreams about helps develop the theme of love's inconstancy or unreliability.

[Exit]
*[**Hermia** leaves the scene]*

Act 3

Act 3 Summary

At the end of act 2, because of Puck's mistake with the magic flower, Lysander fell in love with Helena and chased after her, abandoning Hermia in the woods. Meanwhile, Titania fell asleep, and Oberon anointed her eyes with juice from the magic flower so she would fall in love with the first thing or person she saw when she woke up.

Act 3 brings the Mechanicals back in and ties them in to the rest of the story by giving Titania her love object. Act 3 also makes Puck's mistake known to Oberon, who must try to straighten things out for the four mixed-up Athenians.

The act opens with the Mechanicals rehearsing their play. Their rehearsal and their misbegotten attempts to improve the play are disastrous, and these circumstances provide much amusement for Puck when he stumbles upon the troupe. With Titania asleep nearby, Puck decides to turn one of the Mechanicals, the blustering braggart Bottom, into Titania's love interest. He surreptitiously places an ass's head on Bottom, scaring away the rest of the Mechanicals. Titania wakes up, sees Bottom, and, thanks to the magic flower's juice, instantly falls madly in love with him.

Puck tells Oberon about Titania and Bottom, and Oberon is pleased. But when Oberon and Puck spot Hermia chasing after Demetrius, demanding to know what has happened to Lysander, Oberon realizes that Puck must have put the love juice on the eyes of the wrong Athenian man. Hermia and Demetrius argue, with Hermia insisting that he must have killed Lysander. Demetrius denies it. When Hermia finally leaves, Demetrius lies down to sleep. Oberon puts the magic flower juice on Demetrius's eyes, and when Helena arrives, pursued by the amorous Lysander, Demetrius falls in love with her, too. Hermia comes back and is shocked to discover that Lysander and Demetrius are both in love with Helena, who is convinced that all three of the others are only making fun of her. The four of them argue until Oberon gets Puck to lead Demetrius and Lysander away and get them lost in the woods. Then they all fall asleep, and Puck puts juice from a different flower onto Lysander's eyes to remove the spell of the first flower, the one that made him fall in love with Helena.

Act 3, Scene 1

The wood, where Titania lies asleep

[Enter **Quince**, **Snug**, **Bottom**, **Flute**, **Snout**, and **Starveling**]

[Quince, Snug, Bottom, Flute, Snout, and Starveling enter the scene]

BOTTOM

1   Are we all met?

Is everyone here?

QUINCE

  Pat, pat; and here's a marvellous convenient place
for our rehearsal. This green plot shall be our
stage, this hawthorn-brake our tiring-house; and we
5 will do it in action as we will do it before the duke.

Quick, quick. Here's a wonderfully convenient place to rehearse. This grassy area will be our stage, this hawthorn bush our dressing room, and we will rehearse full out, as if this were the performance in front of the duke.

BOTTOM

  Peter Quince,—

Peter Quince—

QUINCE

  What sayest thou, bully Bottom?

What is it, Bottom, my fine fellow?

BOTTOM

  There are things in this comedy of Pyramus and
Thisby that will never please. First, Pyramus must

10 draw a sword to kill himself; which the ladies
    cannot abide. How answer you that?

There are things in this comedy, Pyramus and Thisby, *that just won't make an audi-*
ence happy. First, Pyramus is supposed to draw a sword to kill himself, which the
ladies won't be able to take.

> This is another of Bottom's verbal mix-ups. By now he's read the play and should
> have seen that it's a tragedy, with the lovers dying at the end, but he still refers
> to it in absolute seriousness as a comedy.

SNOUT

By'r lakin, a parlous fear.

By our ladykin, that's a perilous fear.

> **lakin:** This word stands in for the name of the Virgin Mary. Note how Shake-
> speare sometimes has the characters referring to Greek gods and goddesses
> and sometimes has them speaking in the voices of sixteenth-century English
> Protestants. The Athenian setting gets fainter and fainter as the play goes on.

STARVELING

I believe we must leave the killing out, when all is done.

I believe we're going to have to leave the killing out, after all.

BOTTOM

Not a whit: I have a device to make all well.
15 Write me a prologue; and let the prologue seem to
    say, we will do no harm with our swords, and that
    Pyramus is not killed indeed; and, for the more
    better assurance, tell them that I, Pyramus, am not
    Pyramus, but Bottom the weaver: this will put them
20 out of fear.

Not at all. I have an idea that will make it work. Write me a prologue, and in the pro-
logue say that we aren't actually killing ourselves with the swords, and that Pyramus

isn't really dead. Even better, tell them that I, Pyramus, am not really Pyramus, but Bottom the Weaver. This way they won't be scared.

Shakespeare always liked to make jokes about the world of the theater, and here he's gently poking fun at amateur theatrical companies. The Mechanicals' concern about distinguishing appearance from reality is also a theme of the play.

QUINCE

Well, we will have such a prologue; and it shall be
written in eight and six.

Okay, we'll have a prologue like that, and it will be written in the measure of eight and six.

---

written in eight and six: It was common for ballads to be written in a pattern of lines alternating between eight syllables and six syllables.

BOTTOM

No, make it two more; let it be written in eight and eight.

No, add two more. Make it eight and eight.

---

written in eight and eight: In an attempt to be extra grand, Bottom recommends a writing style that is actually less grand.

SNOUT

Will not the ladies be afeard of the lion?

Won't the ladies be scared of the lion?

STARVELING

25   I fear it, I promise you.

To be honest, that's what I'm worried about.

BOTTOM

> Masters, you ought to consider with yourselves: to
> bring in—God shield us!—a lion among ladies, is a
> most dreadful thing; for there is not a more fearful
> wild-fowl than your lion living; and we ought to
> 30 look to 't.

> *Gentlemen, you ought to think about this. Bringing—God help us!—a lion in among*
> *the ladies is a terrible thing because there's no wild bird scarier than a lion. We*
> *should keep that in mind.*

Shakespeare may have based this idea about replacing the lion on an actual
event that occurred in Scotland in 1594, when a tame lion was supposed to pull
a chariot during a royal entertainment but was replaced by a human being, for fear
of frightening the audience; see G. Blakemore Evans and J. J. M. Tobin, eds. **The
Riverside Shakespeare**, 2nd ed., vol. 1 (Boston: Houghton Mifflin, 1997), 265.

SNOUT

> Therefore another prologue must tell he is not a lion.

> *Then we'll have to have another prologue that explains that he is not really a lion.*

BOTTOM

> Nay, you must name his name, and half his face must
> be seen through the lion's neck: and he himself
> must speak through, saying thus, or to the same
> 35 defect,—"Ladies,"—or "Fair-ladies—I would wish
> You,"—or "I would request you,"—or "I would
> entreat you,—not to fear, not to tremble: my life
> for yours. If you think I come hither as a lion, it
> were pity of my life: no I am no such thing; I am a
> 40 man as other men are;" and there indeed let him name
> his name, and tell them plainly he is Snug the joiner.

> *No, that's not enough. You have to say his name, and half of his face will have to be*
> *visible through the lion's costume, and he himself will have to say this, or something*
> *to this defect: "Ladies," or "Fair ladies—I would wish you," or "I would request you,"*

or "I would beg you not to fear, not to tremble. I would give my life for yours. If you think I came here as a lion, it would put my life in danger. No, I am no such thing. I am a man, the same as other men." And then he can say his name, and say right out that he is Snug the Joiner.

---

defect: Bottom means ***effect.***

QUINCE

Well it shall be so. But there is two hard things;
that is, to bring the moonlight into a chamber; for,
you know, Pyramus and Thisby meet by moonlight.

All right, we'll do that. But there are two other problems—for one, how to make the moon shine into the room. Because, as you know, Pyramus and Thisby meet by moonlight.

SNOUT

45   Doth the moon shine that night we play our play?

Will the moon be shining on the night we perform our play?

BOTTOM

A calendar, a calendar! look in the almanac; find
out moonshine, find out moonshine.

A calendar, a calendar! Look in the almanac! Find out when the moon will be shining, find out when the moon will be shining.

An almanac would have shown the phases of the moon.

QUINCE

Yes, it doth shine that night.

*[**Quince** consults an almanac] Yes, it will be shining that night.*

BOTTOM

> Why then, may you leave a casement of the great
> 50 chamber window, where we play, open, and the moon
> may shine in at the casement.

Well, then, you can leave a window open in the room where we're performing, and the moon can shine in through the window.

QUINCE

> Ay; or else one must come in with a bush of thorns
> and a lanthorn, and say he comes to disfigure, or to
> present, the person of Moonshine. Then, there is
> 55 another thing: we must have a wall in the great
> chamber; for Pyramus and Thisby, says the story, did
> talk through the chink of a wall.

Yes. Either that or somebody will have to come in carrying a bundle of thorns and a lantern and say that he comes to disfigure, or to present, the person of Moonshine. Then there's another problem. We need a wall in the great chamber, since the story says that Pyramus and Thisby spoke to each other through a hole in the wall.

In English folklore, the man in the moon was often shown as an old man carrying a bundle of thorns on his back. "Disfigure" is Quince's word mix-up for **prefigure**, or suggest.

SNOUT

> You can never bring in a wall. What say you, Bottom?

You can't bring a wall in. What do you think, Bottom?

BOTTOM

> Some man or other must present Wall: and let him
> 60 have some plaster, or some loam, or some rough-cast
> about him, to signify wall; and let him hold his
> fingers thus, and through that cranny shall Pyramus
> and Thisby whisper.

Somebody will have to pretend to be a wall. He can have some kind of plaster or mud or rough-cast on him to show that he's a wall. Then he can hold his fingers like this, to make the crack for Pyramus and Thisby to whisper through.

rough-cast: This was a mixture of plaster and pebbles.

QUINCE

If that may be, then all is well. Come, sit down,
65 every mother's son, and rehearse your parts.
Pyramus, you begin: when you have spoken your
speech, enter into that brake: and so every one
according to his cue.

If we can do that, then everything will work out fine. Come on, sit down, all of you, and rehearse your parts. Pyramus, you start. When you've said your lines, walk into that bush, and all the rest of you will go there, too, whenever it's time for you to leave the stage.

[Enter **Puck** behind]
[**Puck**, *unseen by the others, enters the scene from the back of the stage*]

PUCK

What hempen home-spuns have we swaggering here,
70 So near the cradle of the fairy queen?
What, a play toward! I'll be an auditor;
An actor too, perhaps, if I see cause.

What kind of rough country folk do we have playing around here, so close to the bed of our fairy queen? Whoa—there's going to be a play? I'll listen in—and join in, too, if it suits my fancy.

hempen home-spuns: Puck means people wearing homemade clothes of cheap, rough hemp cloth.

QUINCE

Speak, Pyramus. Thisby, stand forth.

Speak, Pyramus. Thisby, go stand over there.

BOTTOM

Thisby, the flowers of odious savours sweet,—

*[**Bottom** speaks as **PYRAMUS**] Thisby, the flowers that have sweet odious smells—*

QUINCE

75 Odours, odours.

Odors, odors.

Odours, odours: Quince is giving Bottom a hint and attempting to correct Bottom's substitution of "odious" (which means "hateful") for "odors"—although what Bottom really should say is **fragrant**.

BOTTOM

—odours savours sweet:
So hath thy breath, my dearest Thisby dear.
But hark, a voice! stay thou but here awhile,
And by and by I will to thee appear.

*[**Bottom** continues speaking as **PYRAMUS**] —sweet odors smells: That's what your breath is like, my dearest Thisby dear. But listen—a voice! Wait here a minute, and I'll be right back.*

[Exit]
*[**Bottom** leaves the scene]*

PUCK

80 [Aside] A stranger Pyramus than e'er played here.

*[**Puck** speaks to himself] That's the strangest Pyramus ever.*

[Exit]
*[**Puck** leaves the scene]*

FLUTE

Must I speak now?

Do I have to speak now?

Flute is very unhappy playing the role of a woman, Thisbe.

QUINCE

Ay, marry, must you; for you must understand he goes
but to see a noise that he heard, and is to come again.

Yes, you certainly do. Because, you see, he's left to check out a noise he heard, and then he'll come back again.

FLUTE

85   Most radiant Pyramus, most lily-white of hue,
Of colour like the red rose on triumphant brier,
Most brisky juvenal and eke most lovely Jew,
As true as truest horse that yet would never tire,
I'll meet thee, Pyramus, at Ninny's tomb.

*[**Flute** speaks as **THISBE**] Brightest Pyramus, with skin of lily-white hue, red like a rose on a thriving bush, lively juvenile and lovely Jew, as faithful as the most faithful and tireless horse, I'll meet you, Pyramus, at Ninny's tomb.*

> **most lovely Jew:** This is an example of the bad poetry in the Mechanicals' play. **Jew** doesn't make sense here, but it's a desperate try for a rhyme with "hue" and an attempted play on the first syllable of "juvenal."

QUINCE

90   "Ninus' tomb," man: why, you must not speak that
yet; that you answer to Pyramus: you speak all your
part at once, cues and all. Pyramus, enter: your cue
is past; it is, "never tire."

That should be "Ninus's tomb," man. But it's not time for you to say that. You're supposed to say that when you answer Pyramus, but you're speaking your lines all at once, even the cues. And, Pyramus, you're supposed to come in here. You missed your cue. It's "tireless horse."

Ninus: In Greek mythology, Ninus is the founder of Ninevah, an ancient city on the Tigris River. Ninus's wife, Semiramis, had a tomb built for him outside Babylon, the city that she built, where the ancient story of Pyramus and Thisbe is set.

FLUTE

O,—As true as truest horse, that yet would
95   never tire.

*Oh.— [**Flute** resumes speaking as **THISBE**] As faithful as the most faithful and tireless horse.*

[Re-enter **Puck**, and **Bottom** with an ass's head]
*[**Puck** reenters the scene; **Bottom** reenters the scene, wearing the head of an ass, which Puck has put on him]*

BOTTOM

If I were fair, Thisby, I were only thine:

*[**Bottom** speaks as **PYRAMUS**] If only I were handsome, Thisby, I would be yours alone.*

Bottom has no idea that he is now wearing the head of an ass.

QUINCE

O monstrous! O strange! we are haunted. Pray,
masters! fly, masters! Help!

It's a monster! We're being haunted! Run, everybody! Help!

[Exeunt **Quince**, **Snug**, **Flute**, **Snout**, and **Starveling**]
*[**Quince**, **Snug**, **Flute**, **Snout**, and **Starveling** leave the scene]*

PUCK

I'll follow you, I'll lead you about a round,
100   Through bog, through bush, through brake, through brier:
Sometime a horse I'll be, sometime a hound,
A hog, a headless bear, sometime a fire;

And neigh, and bark, and grunt, and roar, and burn,
Like horse, hound, hog, bear, fire, at every turn.

I'll follow the whole bunch of you, I'll chase you around in circles, through the mud, through the bushes, through the bracken ferns, through the briar. Sometimes I'll seem like a horse, or a dog, or a hog, or a headless bear, and sometimes like a fire. I'll neigh like a horse, and bark like a dog, and grunt like a hog, and roar like a bear, and burn like a fire, wherever you turn.

[Exit]
*[**Puck** leaves the scene]*

BOTTOM

105   Why do they run away? this is a knavery of them to
make me afeard.

Why are they running away? This is some kind of trick to try to scare me.

[Re-enter **Snout**]
*[**Snout** reenters the scene]*

SNOUT

O Bottom, thou art changed! what do I see on thee?

Oh, Bottom, you've been transformed! What is that on you?

BOTTOM

What do you see? you see an asshead of your own, do
you?

What are you looking at? Are you seeing things? Maybe some asinine thing you dreamed up yourself?

Bottom tries to insult Snout, but he nails the problem—Snout does indeed see something asinine.

[Exit **Snout**]
*[**Snout** leaves the scene]*

[Re-enter **Quince**]

*[**Quince** reenters the scene]*

QUINCE

110 Bless thee, Bottom! bless thee! thou art
translated.

God help you, Bottom! God help you! You've been transformed!

This change in Bottom demonstrates one of the major themes of the play—transformation—as Bottom now becomes a mixture of man and beast. Then again, Puck's choice of animal head is very appropriate, since Bottom has always been an ass.

[Exit]

*[**Quince** leaves the scene]*

BOTTOM

I see their knavery: this is to make an ass of me;
to fright me, if they could. But I will not stir
from this place, do what they can: I will walk up

115 and down here, and I will sing, that they shall hear
I am not afraid.
[Sings] "The ousel cock so black of hue,
With orange-tawny bill,
The throstle with his note so true,

120 The wren with little quill,—"

*I see their tricks. They're trying to make an ass of me to see if they can frighten me. I won't leave this place, though, no matter what they do. I will walk up and down here, and I will sing, so they'll know I'm not afraid. [**Bottom** sings] "The blackbird of so dark a color, with his orange-brown beak, the song thrush with his perfect song, the wren with voice so weak—"*

---

this is to make an ass of me: This is an example of dramatic irony, with the audience knowing more than the characters know. In this situation, the words of the characters take on extra meaning for the audience. Bottom is simply complaining that his friends are trying to make a fool (an ass) of him, but the audience finds this funny because Bottom has indeed been made into an ass.

TITANIA

[Waking] What angel awakes me from my flowerly bed?

[Titania wakes up] What angelic voice is this that wakes me from my bed of flowers?

BOTTOM

[Sings] "The finch, the sparrow and the lark,
The plain-song cuckoo gray,
Whose note full many a man doth mark,
125 And dares not answer nay;—"
[Speaks] for, indeed, who would set his wit to so foolish
a bird? who would give a bird the lie, though he cry
"cuckoo" never so?

[Bottom sings] "The finch, the sparrow, and the lark, the plain song of the gray cuckoo, whose full song many men do hear but do not dare say no to—" [Bottom speaks] Of course they don't answer. Who'd answer such a silly bird? Who'd accuse the bird of lying, even though he cries out "Cuckoo"?

The cuckoo bird is a play on the word **cuckold**, which means a man whose wife has cheated on him. The cuckoo's song was supposed to be a warning to a man that he had been cuckolded.

TITANIA

I pray thee, gentle mortal, sing again:
130 Mine ear is much enamour'd of thy note;
So is mine eye enthralled to thy shape;
And thy fair virtue's force perforce doth move me
On the first view to say, to swear, I love thee.

Please, sweet man, sing again. My ears are in love with the sound of your voice. My eyes are equally enchanted by your figure, and the power of your fine qualities has the force to make me, with one look, say and swear that I love you.

The idea that Titania can fall in love so easily, and with something so ridiculous, plays into the theme of love's irrationality.

BOTTOM

> Methinks, mistress, you should have little reason
> 135   for that: and yet, to say the truth, reason and
> love keep little company together now-a-days; the
> more the pity that some honest neighbours will not
> make them friends. Nay, I can gleek upon occasion.

I think, lady, that you should have little reason to feel that way, and yet, to be honest, reason and love don't often go together these days. Too bad someone won't get them together! Oh, yes, I can make jokes sometimes.

Bottom states another of the play's themes—that love and reason, or clear thinking, don't often go together. Love doesn't make sense, and love makes people a little crazy.

TITANIA

> Thou art as wise as thou art beautiful.

You are as smart as you are good-looking.

Titania has just handed out what is basically everyone's ideal compliment—and to a country bumpkin wearing an ass's head.

BOTTOM

> 140   Not so, neither: but if I had wit enough to get out
> of this wood, I have enough to serve mine own turn.

No, that's not true. But if I were smart enough to find my way out of this forest, that would be smart enough for me.

TITANIA

> Out of this wood do not desire to go:
> Thou shalt remain here, whether thou wilt or no.

I am a spirit of no common rate;
145 The summer still doth tend upon my state;
And I do love thee: therefore, go with me;
I'll give thee fairies to attend on thee,
And they shall fetch thee jewels from the deep,
And sing while thou on pressed flowers dost sleep;
150 And I will purge thy mortal grossness so
That thou shalt like an airy spirit go.
Peaseblossom! Cobweb! Moth! and Mustardseed!

Don't say you want to leave this forest. You shall stay here, whether you want to or not. I am a fairy of no ordinary means. The summer is one of my servants and follows me wherever I go. I do love you. So come with me. I'll have fairies wait on you, and they will bring you jewels from the bottom of the sea, and sing to you while you sleep on a bed of flowers. I will change your human body and take away your mortality so you will live forever, the way we fairies do. Peaseblossom! Cobweb! Moth! And Mustardseed!

[Enter **Peaseblossom**, **Cobweb**, **Moth**, and **Mustardseed**]

*[**Peaseblossom**, **Cobweb**, **Moth**, and **Mustardseed** enter the scene]*

PEASEBLOSSOM

Ready.

Here!

COBWEB

And I.

Me, too!

MOTH

155 And I.

Me, too!

MUSTARDSEED

And I.

Me, too!

ALL

Where shall we go?

Where should we go?

TITANIA

Be kind and courteous to this gentleman;
Hop in his walks and gambol in his eyes;
160 Feed him with apricoks and dewberries,
With purple grapes, green figs, and mulberries;
The honey-bags steal from the humble-bees,
And for night-tapers crop their waxen thighs
And light them at the fiery glow-worm's eyes,
165 To have my love to bed and to arise;
And pluck the wings from painted butterflies
To fan the moonbeams from his sleeping eyes:
Nod to him, elves, and do him courtesies.

Be sweet and gentle to this man. Skip on his feet and dance in his eyes. Feed him apricots, dewberries, purple grapes, green figs, and mulberries. Steal the honey bags from honeybees and make candles from the bees' wax, then light them with the fire of glowworms' eyes to lead my love to bed and help him wake. Take the wings of brightly colored butterflies to fan the sleep out of his drowsy eyes. Bow to him, fairies, and treat him well.

PEASEBLOSSOM

Hail, mortal!

Hail, mortal!

COBWEB

170 Hail!

Hail!

MOTH

Hail!

Hail!

MUSTARDSEED

Hail!

Hail!

BOTTOM

I cry your worship's mercy, heartily: I beseech your
worship's name.

*[**Bottom** speaks to **Cobweb**] I beg your grace's pardon. Please tell me your name.*

COBWEB

175   Cobweb.

Cobweb.

BOTTOM

I shall desire you of more acquaintance, good Master
Cobweb: if I cut my finger, I shall make bold with
you. Your name, honest gentleman?

*I will need to get to know you better, good Sir Cobweb. If I cut my finger, I'll be all
over you. [**Bottom** speaks to **Peaseblossom**] Your name, honest fellow?*

---

if I cut my finger: Cobwebs were believed to put a stop to bleeding.

PEASEBLOSSOM

Peaseblossom.

Peaseblossom.

BOTTOM

180   I pray you, commend me to Mistress Squash, your
mother, and to Master Peascod, your father. Good
Master Peaseblossom, I shall desire you of more
acquaintance too. Your name, I beseech you, sir?

*Please send my greetings to Mrs. Squash, your mother, and to Mr. Peascod, your father. Good Mr. Peaseblossom, I will want to get to know you better. [**Bottom** speaks to **Mustardseed**] Your name, I beg of you, sir?*

A squash is an unripe pea pod, and a peascod is a ripe pea pod.

MUSTARDSEED

Mustardseed.

Mustardseed.

BOTTOM

185   Good Master Mustardseed, I know your patience well:
that same cowardly, giant-like ox-beef hath
devoured many a gentleman of your house: I promise
you your kindred had made my eyes water ere now. I
desire your more acquaintance, good Master
190   Mustardseed.

Good Mr. Mustardseed, I know your suffering well. Many a giant slab of beef has been seasoned with men from your family. I swear, your spicy relatives have often made my eyes water. I hope to get to know you better, good Mr. Mustardseed.

TITANIA

Come, wait upon him; lead him to my bower.
The moon methinks looks with a watery eye;
And when she weeps, weeps every little flower,
Lamenting some enforced chastity.
195   Tie up my love's tongue. Bring him silently.

Come, wait upon him. Lead him to my flowery bed. I think the moon is looking down tearfully. When she weeps, dewdrops fall on every little flower, making them weep, too, because of the violence done to some pure maiden. Silence my lover. Bring him quietly.

---

enforced chastity: This phrase doesn't mean an involuntary state of abstinence. Instead, it means a state of chastity, or purity, that has been stolen by force ("enforced"). In other words, the phrase alludes to the violation of a virgin. The goddess of the moon is also the goddess of virtue, and so the image is that of the moon weeping.

[Exeunt]
[Everyone leaves the scene]

Act 3, Scene 2

Another part of the wood

[Enter **Oberon**, solus]

*[**Oberon** enters the scene, alone]*

OBERON

1   I wonder if Titania be awaked;
    Then, what it was that next came in her eye,
    Which she must dote on in extremity.

I wonder if Titania is awake yet—and, if so, what she saw when she woke up that she now has to be madly in love with.

[Enter **Puck**]

*[**Puck** enters the scene]*

    Here comes my messenger.
5   How now, mad spirit!
    What night-rule now about this haunted grove?

Here's my messenger. How's it going, crazy sprite? What mad sport have you been having in this grove where we so often find ourselves?

---

night-rule: This means night activity, night play, or any work commonly done at night.

PUCK

    My mistress with a monster is in love.
    Near to her close and consecrated bower,
    While she was in her dull and sleeping hour,
10   A crew of patches, rude mechanicals,
    That work for bread upon Athenian stalls,
    Were met together to rehearse a play
    Intended for great Theseus' nuptial-day.
    The shallowest thick-skin of that barren sort,
15   Who Pyramus presented, in their sport

Forsook his scene and enter'd in a brake
When I did him at this advantage take,
An ass's nole I fixed on his head:
Anon his Thisbe must be answered,
20 And forth my mimic comes. When they him spy,
As wild geese that the creeping fowler eye,
Or russet-pated choughs, many in sort,
Rising and cawing at the gun's report,
Sever themselves and madly sweep the sky,
25 So, at his sight, away his fellows fly;
And, at our stamp, here o'er and o'er one falls;
He murder cries and help from Athens calls.
Their sense thus weak, lost with their fears thus strong,
Made senseless things begin to do them wrong;
30 For briers and thorns at their apparel snatch;
Some sleeves, some hats, from yielders all things catch.
I led them on in this distracted fear,
And left sweet Pyramus translated there:
When in that moment, so it came to pass,
35 Titania waked and straightway loved an ass.

My lady is in love with a monster! While she slept in her secret flowery bed, a group of rough workmen, who make their living selling their work at the market, came together to rehearse a play that they hope to perform on great Theseus's wedding day. When the one who played Pyramus, the biggest blockhead in that parade of idiots, exited a scene and went into the bushes, I put an ass's head on him. Then, when his Thisbe called him, my actor went back to them. When they saw him, they ran away as fast as wild geese or crows fly into the air at the sound of the hunter's gun. At the sound of my foot stamping, one of them fell over himself, calling out, "Murder!" and crying for help from Athens. They were so scared, they lost their senses and became frightened of everything around them—the briars and thorns pulling at their clothes, grabbing at their sleeves and hats. I chased them away and left sweet Pyramus transformed there. Then, at that moment, Titania woke up and fell in love with an ass.

Athenian stalls: Workers like these "rude mechanicals," as Puck characterized the tradesmen, would have sold their products in stalls, or booths, at an open market. Note that it is Puck who gives the Mechanicals their name in this play.

nole: This word means "head."

senseless things: These are things like trees, branches, and rocks, which don't have the ability to think.

Recall that when Puck placed the ass's head on Bottom, both characters were offstage. Therefore, this account from Puck is the first explanation that the audience receives of how Bottom came to be wearing the head of an ass.

OBERON

This falls out better than I could devise.
But hast thou yet latch'd the Athenian's eyes
With the love-juice, as I did bid thee do?

That's even better than what I hoped for. But did you also put the flower's juice on the Athenian's eyes, as I asked you to do?

PUCK

I took him sleeping, —that is finish'd too, —
40   And the Athenian woman by his side:
That, when he waked, of force she must be eyed.

I found him sleeping—so that's done, too. The Athenian woman was sleeping nearby, so when he woke up, she had to be the first thing he saw.

[Enter **Hermia** and **Demetrius**]
*[**Hermia** and **Demetrius** enter the scene]*

OBERON

Stand close: this is the same Athenian.

*[**Oberon** speaks to **Puck**] Stay near me. That's the Athenian.*

PUCK

This is the woman, but not this the man.

That's the woman, all right, but that's not the same man.

DEMETRIUS

O, why rebuke you him that loves you so?
45   Lay breath so bitter on your bitter foe.

Why do you speak so harshly to the one who loves you so much? Save your cruel words for your worst enemy.

HERMIA

Now I but chide; but I should use thee worse
For thou, I fear, hast given me cause to curse,
If thou hast slain Lysander in his sleep,
Being o'er shoes in blood, plunge in the deep,
50   And kill me too.
The sun was not so true unto the day
As he to me: would he have stolen away
From sleeping Hermia? I'll believe as soon
This whole earth may be bored and that the moon
55   May through the centre creep and so displease
Her brother's noontide with Antipodes.
It cannot be but thou hast murder'd him;
So should a murderer look, so dead, so grim.

This is just gentle scolding, but I should be treating you much worse because I'm worried you've given me good reason to curse you. If you killed Lysander in his sleep, then you're already ankle-deep in blood, so you might as well kill me, too. The sun wasn't as faithful to the day as he was to me. Would he have sneaked away from me in the middle of the night? I'll believe that as soon as the moon drops through the center of the earth and comes out at the bottom, displeasing her brother sun's noontime down there. The only possible explanation is that you murdered him. You even look like a murderer—deathly pale and grim.

stolen away from sleeping Hermia: Here is more dramatic irony—Hermia swears that Lysander loves her and would never leave her, but the audience knows that he has run off to chase after Helena, his new love.

displease her brother's noontide: The sun and the moon are imagined here as brother and sister. Hermia is envisioning the chaos that would result if the moon fell from the night, at the top of the world, down to the bottom of the world, where it's day.

DEMETRIUS

> So should the murder'd look, and so should I,
> 60   Pierced through the heart with your stern cruelty:
> Yet you, the murderer, look as bright, as clear,
> As yonder Venus in her glimmering sphere.

> *The murder victim would look this way, and so would I, since I've been pierced*
> *through the heart by your cruelty. Yet you, the murderer, look as bright and clear as*
> *faraway Venus hanging in the sky.*

HERMIA

> What's this to my Lysander? where is he?
> Ah, good Demetrius, wilt thou give him me?

> *What does this have to do with my Lysander? Where is he? Please, good Demetrius,*
> *will you show me where he is?*

DEMETRIUS

> 65   I had rather give his carcass to my hounds.

> *I would rather feed his body to my dogs.*

HERMIA

> Out, dog! out, cur! thou drivest me past the bounds
> Of maiden's patience. Hast thou slain him, then?
> Henceforth be never number'd among men!
> O, once tell true, tell true, even for my sake!
> 70   Durst thou have look'd upon him being awake,
> And hast thou kill'd him sleeping? O brave touch!
> Could not a worm, an adder, do so much?
> An adder did it; for with doubler tongue
> Than thine, thou serpent, never adder stung.

> *Get away, you dog! Go away, you mongrel! You have pushed me past the bounds of*
> *any girl's patience. So you've killed him? Then from this day forward, you'll never*
> *again belong to the human race. Oh, for once, tell me the truth, please tell me the*
> *truth—just do it for me. You hardly dared to look at him while he was awake, and*
> *yet you killed him while he was sleeping? Oh, how noble! How does that make you*

different from a worm or a poisonous snake? But it was a snake that did it—no snake's forked tongue ever delivered more poison than yours.

---

doubler tongue: The forked, or split, tongue of the snake represents deceit. The tongue's two forks allow the snake, or speaker, to say two different things at the same time. Snake imagery also occurs elsewhere in the play, as in the fairies' song and Hermia's dream (both in act 2, scene 2).

DEMETRIUS

75   You spend your passion on a misprised mood:
I am not guilty of Lysander's blood;
Nor is he dead, for aught that I can tell.

You're getting all worked up over nothing. I didn't kill Lysander. He's not even dead, as far as I know.

HERMIA

I pray thee, tell me then that he is well.

I beg you, then, tell me that he's all right.

DEMETRIUS

An if I could, what should I get therefore?

If I could tell you that, what would be in it for me?

HERMIA

80   A privilege never to see me more.
And from thy hated presence part I so:
See me no more, whether he be dead or no.

The gift of never seeing me again. I'm leaving your loathsome presence. Stay out of my sight, whether he's dead or alive.

[Exit]
*[**Hermia** leaves the scene]*

DEMETRIUS

> There is no following her in this fierce vein:
> Here therefore for a while I will remain.
85   So sorrow's heaviness doth heavier grow
> For debt that bankrupt sleep doth sorrow owe:
> Which now in some slight measure it will pay,
> If for his tender here I make some stay.

> *There's no point in going after her while she's so worked up. I'll wait here for a while.*
> *Lack of sleep makes sadness feel even worse. I'll pay off my sleep debt with a nap*
> *right here.*

> [Lies down and sleeps]
> *[**Demetrius** lies down and falls asleep]*

OBERON

> What hast thou done? thou hast mistaken quite
90   And laid the love-juice on some true-love's sight:
> Of thy misprision must perforce ensue
> Some true love turn'd and not a false turn'd true.

> *[**Oberon** speaks to **Puck**] What have you done? You've made a mistake and put the*
> *love juice on the eyes of someone who was already in love with the right person.*
> *Your mistake means that someone's true love has turned false, and the false love*
> *hasn't turned true.*

PUCK

> Then fate o'er-rules, that, one man holding troth,
> A million fail, confounding oath on oath.

> *Then fate wins out. For every man who stays true, a million more fail and*
> *break their promises.*

> Mischievous Puck, who doesn't care about people's feelings or what is right,
> shrugs away his mistake by suggesting that it happened because it was fated
> to happen.

OBERON

95 About the wood go swifter than the wind,
And Helena of Athens look thou find:
All fancy-sick she is and pale of cheer,
With sighs of love, that costs the fresh blood dear:
By some illusion see thou bring her here:
100 I'll charm his eyes against she do appear.

Race through this wood, faster than the wind, and find Helena of Athens. She's pale with lovesickness, sighing, for lack of love has drained the color from her cheeks. Then use some trick to get her over here, and I'll put the spell on this sleeping man's eyes when she's in front of him.

costs the fresh blood dear: It was believed that a sigh drains a drop of blood from the heart, a notion that goes with the idea that paleness indicates sadness or melancholy.

PUCK

I go, I go; look how I go,
Swifter than arrow from the Tartar's bow.

I'm going, I'm going. See? Faster than an arrow from a Tartar's bow.

The Tartars, fabled for their skill as archers, belonged to the Mongol empire of Genghis Khan.

[Exit]
[***Puck** leaves the scene*]

OBERON

Flower of this purple dye,
Hit with Cupid's archery,
105 Sink in apple of his eye.
When his love he doth espy,
Let her shine as gloriously
As the Venus of the sky.
When thou wakest, if she be by,

110 Beg of her for remedy.

*[**Oberon** speaks to the flower] Purple flower, pierced by Cupid's arrow, sink into the center of this man's eye. Then, when he sees his love, let her glow as brilliantly as Venus in the sky. [**Oberon** speaks to the sleeping **Demetrius**] When you wake, if she's nearby, beg her to cure you with her love.*

[Re-enter **Puck**]
*[**Puck** reenters the scene]*

PUCK

Captain of our fairy band,
Helena is here at hand;
And the youth, mistook by me,
Pleading for a lover's fee.
115 Shall we their fond pageant see?
Lord, what fools these mortals be!

Helena is right here, Captain, and so is that young man I accidentally caused to fall in love with her. He's pleading for his rights as her lover. Shall we watch their silly show? Lord, these humans are fools!

OBERON

Stand aside: the noise they make
Will cause Demetrius to awake.

Step aside—they're making so much noise, they're going to wake Demetrius.

PUCK

Then will two at once woo one;
120 That must needs be sport alone;
And those things do best please me
That befal preposterously.

Then the two of them will both end up chasing after her—that alone will be plenty of fun. I love it when disorder rules.

[Enter **Lysander** and **Helena**]
*[**Lysander** and **Helena** enter the scene]*

LYSANDER

Why should you think that I should woo in scorn?
Scorn and derision never come in tears:
125   Look, when I vow, I weep; and vows so born,
In their nativity all truth appears,
How can these things in me seem scorn to you,
Bearing the badge of faith, to prove them true?

Why would you think I'm swearing my love to you just to make fun of you? Mockery isn't about tears. I'm swearing my love to you, and I'm crying. See? Vows born of tears are the most sincere. How can this seem like a joke to you, when everything I do is a sign of true faithfulness?

HELENA

You do advance your cunning more and more.
130   When truth kills truth, O devilish-holy fray!
These vows are Hermia's: will you give her o'er?
Weigh oath with oath, and you will nothing weigh:
Your vows to her and me, put in two scales,
Will even weigh, and both as light as tales.

The more you speak, the more you give your tricks away. Two truths can't be true, so when one truth kills the other, oh, the hell that will break loose! The love you've sworn to me, you swore to Hermia. Are you planning to drop her? Weigh each of your two vows against the other, and you'll come up with nothing. Put your vows to me on one scale and the vows you made to her on another, and they'll both be even—both as light as lies.

LYSANDER

135   I had no judgment when to her I swore.

I wasn't thinking when I swore my love to her.

HELENA

Nor none, in my mind, now you give her o'er.

And, in my opinion, you're also not thinking now that you're dropping her.

LYSANDER

Demetrius loves her, and he loves not you.

Demetrius loves her, and he doesn't love you.

[Awakening]
[Demetrius wakes up]

DEMETRIUS

O, Helena, goddess, nymph, perfect, divine!
To what, my love, shall I compare thine eyne?
140   Crystal is muddy. O, how ripe in show
Thy lips, those kissing cherries, tempting grow!
That pure congealed white, high Taurus snow,
Fann'd with the eastern wind, turns to a crow
When thou hold'st up thy hand: O, let me kiss
145   This princess of pure white, this seal of bliss!

[Demetrius speaks to Helena] Oh Helena, a goddess, you perfect and divine nymph. My love, to what can I compare your eyes? Crystals are muddy next to them. Oh, your lips are so ripe, as tempting as fresh cherries! That pure snow found on top of the Taurus mountains, chilled by the eastern winds, looks black in comparison to your hand. Oh, let me kiss that pure white hand, which promises such joy!

---

thine eyne: Demetrius, with the juice from the magic flower on his eyes (or "eyne"), wakes up, sees Helena, falls in love with her—and tells her all about it in rhyming couplets of iambic pentameter.

Taurus: This is the name of a mountain range in what is now southern Turkey.

princess of pure white: During the Renaissance, pure white skin represented virtue and modesty and was therefore considered a sign of beauty. Women even wore white powder to make themselves look paler. Unfortunately, though, the most common type of white powder for the face included lead, which is toxic.

HELENA

O spite! O hell! I see you all are bent
To set against me for your merriment:
If you were civil and knew courtesy,

You would not do me thus much injury.

150 Can you not hate me, as I know you do,
But you must join in souls to mock me too?
If you were men, as men you are in show,
You would not use a gentle lady so;
To vow, and swear, and superpraise my parts,

155 When I am sure you hate me with your hearts.
You both are rivals, and love Hermia;
And now both rivals, to mock Helena:
A trim exploit, a manly enterprise,
To conjure tears up in a poor maid's eyes

160 With your derision! none of noble sort
Would so offend a virgin, and extort
A poor soul's patience, all to make you sport.

Oh, such spitefulness! So hellish! I see you have both decided to make me the target of your jokes. If you were decent and understood kindness, you wouldn't hurt me this way. It's not enough that you hate me, as I know you do, but now you've joined together to make fun of me? If you were real men, not just pretending to be men, you would not treat a harmless girl this way. To make such promises, and swear your love to me, and overpraise every part of me, when I know that you hate me with all your hearts! You are both rivals for the love of Hermia, and now you act like rivals for me, just to mock me. A fine thing to do, truly manly behavior, making fun of a poor girl and making her cry? No one who had any kind of nobility would injure a girl and try her patience just for fun.

Helena doubts what she sees—and the question of appearances versus reality is one of the play's important themes.

LYSANDER

You are unkind, Demetrius; be not so;
For you love Hermia; this you know I know:

165 And here, with all good will, with all my heart,
In Hermia's love I yield you up my part:
And yours of Helena to me bequeath,
Whom I do love and will do till my death.

You're so mean, Demetrius. Don't act this way. You love Hermia. You know I know that. So here, with all my best wishes, with all of my heart, I give up my love of Hermia for your sake, and you can let me take Helena, since I will love her until I die.

HELENA

Never did mockers waste more idle breath.

No two jokers ever wasted so much breath.

DEMETRIUS

170   Lysander, keep thy Hermia; I will none:
If e'er I loved her, all that love is gone.
My heart to her but as guest-wise sojourn'd,
And now to Helen is it home return'd,
There to remain.

Lysander, keep your Hermia. I don't want her. If I ever loved her, that love is gone. It's as if my heart had gone on a little vacation to Hermia, and now it has returned home to Helena, forever.

LYSANDER

175   Helen, it is not so.

Helena, that's not true.

DEMETRIUS

Disparage not the faith thou dost not know,
Lest, to thy peril, thou aby it dear.
Look, where thy love comes; yonder is thy dear.

Don't dismiss true love that you don't understand, or you'll have to pay for that insult. Look, there's your love—she's over there.

---

aby: This word means to pay or atone for something.

[Re-enter **Hermia**]
*[**Hermia** reenters the scene]*

HERMIA

> Dark night, that from the eye his function takes,
> 180   The ear more quick of apprehension makes;
> Wherein it doth impair the seeing sense,
> It pays the hearing double recompense.
> Thou art not by mine eye, Lysander, found;
> Mine ear, I thank it, brought me to thy sound
> 185   But why unkindly didst thou leave me so?

Darkness makes it hard to see, but it makes the ears more alert. Where sight is weakened, hearing becomes doubly strong. I didn't see you, Lysander, but, thanks to my ears, I heard you. Now, why did you leave me so cruelly?

LYSANDER

> Why should he stay, whom love doth press to go?

Why should someone stay, when love tells him to go?

HERMIA

> What love could press Lysander from my side?

What love would tell you to leave me?

LYSANDER

> Lysander's love, that would not let him bide,
> Fair Helena, who more engilds the night
> 190   Than all you fiery oes and eyes of light.
> Why seek'st thou me? could not this make thee know,
> The hate I bear thee made me leave thee so?

My love who wouldn't let me stay there—lovely Helena, who brings more beauty to the night than all the circles of stars. Why are you looking for me? Couldn't you figure out that it was my hatred for you that made me leave you?

---

oes and eyes of light: The stars are depicted here as round objects (like the letter **o**) that are made of light. "Eyes" follows as a pun on the letter *l*.

HERMIA

You speak not as you think: it cannot be.

You don't know what you're saying. This can't be true.

HELENA

Lo, she is one of this confederacy!
195　Now I perceive they have conjoin'd all three
To fashion this false sport, in spite of me.
Injurious Hermia! most ungrateful maid!
Have you conspired, have you with these contrived
To bait me with this foul derision?
200　Is all the counsel that we two have shared,
The sisters' vows, the hours that we have spent,
When we have chid the hasty-footed time
For parting us, — O, is it all forgot?
All school-days' friendship, childhood innocence?
205　We, Hermia, like two artificial gods,
Have with our needles created both one flower,
Both on one sampler, sitting on one cushion,
Both warbling of one song, both in one key,
As if our hands, our sides, voices and minds,
210　Had been incorporate. So we grow together,
Like to a double cherry, seeming parted,
But yet an union in partition;
Two lovely berries moulded on one stem;
So, with two seeming bodies, but one heart;
215　Two of the first, like coats in heraldry,
Due but to one and crowned with one crest.
And will you rent our ancient love asunder,
To join with men in scorning your poor friend?
It is not friendly, 'tis not maidenly:
220　Our sex, as well as I, may chide you for it,
Though I alone do feel the injury.

Oh, she's in on their joke. Now I see it—the three of them are conspiring in this mean little game just to upset me. Cruel Hermia, you ungrateful girl! Have you plotted with them to find a way to torment me? Have you forgotten all the secrets we've shared? How we were like sisters? The hours that we spent together, and how we cursed time when we had to separate? Oh, did you forget all that? All the friendship of our school days, our innocent childhood? We were like two gods, able to use our needles to create one flower on the same sampler, sharing a cushion, singing one song in the same key, as if our hands, our sides, our voices and minds were parts of the same whole. So we grew up together, like a double cherry that looks like two separate pieces but is really bound together. Two beautiful berries, formed on the same stem. It seemed as if we had two bodies, but we shared one heart, like a double coat on a heraldic shield, one that belongs to two people but is crowned with one crest. Now will you tear our longtime love apart just to side with two men making fun of your poor old friend? That's unkind, it's not something a good girl would do. All women, and not just myself, should scold you for these actions, even though I'm the only one who's actually getting hurt.

> **like two artificial gods:** A sampler was a piece of embroidery with which girls practiced their sewing. Helena compares herself and Hermia to gods because when they embroidered flowers on a sampler, they created those flowers just as the gods create real flowers.
>
> **heraldry:** This was the art of creating a coat of arms, which represented a family and its rank. Helena describes two coats of arms united under one crown to show that they are bound together.

HERMIA

I am amazed at your passionate words.
I scorn you not: it seems that you scorn me.

I'm shocked by your angry words. I'm not scorning you. I think you're scorning me.

HELENA

     Have you not set Lysander, as in scorn,
225 To follow me and praise my eyes and face?
     And made your other love, Demetrius,
     Who even but now did spurn me with his foot,
     To call me goddess, nymph, divine and rare,
     Precious, celestial? Wherefore speaks he this
230 To her he hates? and wherefore doth Lysander
     Deny your love, so rich within his soul,

And tender me, forsooth, affection,
But by your setting on, by your consent?
What thought I be not so in grace as you,
235 So hung upon with love, so fortunate,
But miserable most, to love unloved?
This you should pity rather than despise.

Haven't you made Lysander mock me by following me and complimenting my eyes and face? And didn't you also make your other love, Demetrius—who just a few minutes ago practically kicked me to the curb—call me goddess, nymph, heavenly, precious, and rare? Why would someone say such things to someone he hates? And why does Lysander say he doesn't love you, when he felt that love so deeply, and then speak to me tenderly, even affectionately? Didn't you put him up to it? And you did this even though you're so beloved, so lucky, and I'm so miserable, loving but unloved? You should pity me rather than hate me.

HERMIA

I understand not what you mean by this.

I have no idea what you're talking about.

HELENA

Ay, do, persever, counterfeit sad looks,
240 Make mouths upon me when I turn my back;
Wink each at other; hold the sweet jest up:
This sport, well carried, shall be chronicled.
If you have any pity, grace, or manners,
You would not make me such an argument.
245 But fare ye well: 'tis partly my own fault;
Which death or absence soon shall remedy.

Oh, sure, go ahead with your fake sad looks while you make faces at me behind my back. Wink at each other, keep the joke going. You've all done such a good job that someone should write this up and put it in a book. If you have any sympathy, courtesy, or manners, you would not pretend to argue over me. But good-bye: though it's partly my fault, my death or departure will soon fix everything.

LYSANDER

Stay, gentle Helena; hear my excuse:
My love, my life, my soul, fair Helena!

*Wait, gentle Helena. Listen to what I have to say. My love, my life, my soul,
beautiful Helena!*

HELENA

O excellent!

Oh, great.

O excellent!: This is the verbal equivalent of a big eye roll.

HERMIA

250   Sweet, do not scorn her so.

*[**Hermia** speaks to **Lysander**] Sweetheart, don't tease her like that.*

DEMETRIUS

If she cannot entreat, I can compel.

*[**Demetrius** speaks to **Lysander**] If she can't make you stop, I will.*

LYSANDER

Thou canst compel no more than she entreat:
Thy threats have no more strength than her weak prayers.
Helen, I love thee; by my life, I do:
255   I swear by that which I will lose for thee,
To prove him false that says I love thee not.

*[**Lysander** speaks to **Demetrius**] You can't make me any more than she can. Your
threats are as weak as her pleas. [**Lysander** speaks to **Helena**] Helena, I swear on
my life that I love you. I swear I would give up my life for you, just to prove that he's
lying when he says I don't love you.*

DEMETRIUS

I say I love thee more than he can do.

I'm telling you, I love you more than he does.

LYSANDER

If thou say so, withdraw, and prove it too.

If that's what you're saying, then put your sword where your mouth is.

DEMETRIUS

Quick, come!

All right. Come on!

HERMIA

260   Lysander, whereto tends all this?

[holds **Lysander** back]

Lysander, why are you doing this?
*[**Hermia** restrains **Lysander**]*

LYSANDER

Away, you Ethiope!

Get away from me, dark one!

Ethiope: Lysander is calling Hermia an Ethiopian, or an African. The implication is that she has dark hair, or darker skin, valued less than light hair and fair skin.

DEMETRIUS

No, no; he'll [...]
Seem to break loose; take on as you would follow,
But yet come not: you are a tame man, go!

*[**Demetrius** speaks to **Hermia**] No, no. Don't hold him back. He'll just pretend that he's struggling to break free from you. He'll act as if he's coming after me, but then he won't. [**Demetrius** speaks to **Lysander**] Get out of here, you coward!*

LYSANDER

265   Hang off, thou cat, thou burr! vile thing, let loose,
Or I will shake thee from me like a serpent!

*[**Lysander** speaks to **Hermia**] Let go, you clinging cat! You thorn! You disgusting creature! Let go of me, or I'll shake you off me like a snake.*

HERMIA

Why are you grown so rude? what change is this?
Sweet love, —

*[**Hermia** speaks to **Lysander**] Why are you being so mean? What has come over you,
my love?*

LYSANDER

Thy love! out, tawny Tartar, out!
270   Out, loathed medicine! hated potion, hence!

*Your love? Go away, brown Tartar, go away! Begone, you loathsome medicine! Go
away, you detestable poison!*

---

tawny Tartar: Again Lysander insults Hermia by comparing her to a darker-
skinned foreigner, someone from the East.

HERMIA

Do you not jest?

You're joking, right?

HELENA

Yes, sooth; and so do you.

Yes, of course he is—and so are you.

LYSANDER

Demetrius, I will keep my word with thee.

Demetrius, I'm not backing down. I will fight you.

DEMETRIUS

> I would I had your bond, for I perceive
275 A weak bond holds you: I'll not trust your word.

> *I wish we had a signed, binding agreement, since I can see the weakness of what's binding you. I won't trust your word.*

> **a weak bond holds you:** Demetrius is saying that Lysander can't be trusted, since he will use Hermia's restraint of him as an excuse not to fight.

LYSANDER

> What, should I hurt her, strike her, kill her dead?
> Although I hate her, I'll not harm her so.

> *So you want me to hurt her? Hit her? Kill her? I hate her, but I'm not going to do her any harm.*

HERMIA

> What, can you do me greater harm than hate?
> Hate me! wherefore? O me! what news, my love!
280 Am not I Hermia? are not you Lysander?
> I am as fair now as I was erewhile.
> Since night you loved me; yet since night you left me:
> Why, then you left me—O, the gods forbid!—
> In earnest, shall I say?

> *[**Hermia** speaks to **Lysander**] How can you possibly do me any greater harm than hating me? Hate me! Why? Oh my! What's going on, my love? Am I not your Hermia? And aren't you my Lysander? I am as beautiful now as I was just a little while ago. When we got here, you loved me, but while I slept, you left me. So you've really left me? Oh, gods forbid!*

LYSANDER

285 Ay, by my life;
> And never did desire to see thee more.
> Therefore be out of hope, of question, of doubt;
> Be certain, nothing truer; 'tis no jest
> That I do hate thee and love Helena.

Yes, that's right, and I swear on my life I don't ever want to see you again. So abandon hope, stop asking questions, and leave your doubts behind. You can rest assured that there is nothing truer than this, and it's no joke—I hate you, and I love Helena.

HERMIA

290   O me! you juggler! you canker-blossom!
You thief of love! what, have you come by night
And stolen my love's heart from him?

*[**Hermia** speaks to **Helena**] Oh my! You cheater! You toxic worm! You thief of love! Did you come sneaking around by dark of night to steal my love's heart?*

juggler! you canker-blossom!: A juggler is a cheat, probably because the word suggests someone who is balancing or juggling two (or more) lovers. A canker blossom is a worm that gets into a flower bud and poisons it. The image is of Helena getting in between Hermia and Lysander and poisoning their love.

stolen my love's heart: Hermia finally realizes that Lysander has dumped her for Helena, and she accuses Helena of stealing his heart. The couples' journey from conflict to love reaches its peak here as they all battle for love.

HELENA

  Fine, i'faith!
Have you no modesty, no maiden shame,
295   No touch of bashfulness? What, will you tear
Impatient answers from my gentle tongue?
Fie, fie! you counterfeit, you puppet, you!

Oh, that's nice! Have you no shame? Are you trying to make me lose my patience and say mean things to you? Curses! You phony! What a puppet you are!

you counterfeit, you puppet: Helena probably uses "puppet" in the sense of an artificial person, to go along with "counterfeit," but Hermia takes it as a jab about her being short. Hermia is typically played by a small actress and Helena by a tall one.

HERMIA

Puppet? why so? ay, that way goes the game.
Now I perceive that she hath made compare
300 Between our statures; she hath urged her height;
And with her personage, her tall personage,
Her height, forsooth, she hath prevail'd with him.
And are you grown so high in his esteem;
Because I am so dwarfish and so low?
305 How low am I, thou painted maypole? speak;
How low am I? I am not yet so low
But that my nails can reach unto thine eyes.

Puppet? Oh, so that's how it's going to be! Now she's comparing our heights. She used her height to win him over. So now you rate so highly in his favor because you are tall and I am short and low to the ground? Well, how low can I go, you painted maypole? Come on, say it—how low can I go? How about this—I'm not so short that I can't reach up and scratch your eyes out!

---

thou painted maypole: On May 1, known as May Day, people in country villages would put up a tall pole, known as a maypole, and decorate it with paint and ribbons. Then they would circle around the maypole, dancing and singing. "Painted" may be a reference to the decorations on a maypole, but Hermia is more likely to be suggesting that Helena is wearing "paint," or makeup. In other words, she owes her looks to makeup, not to nature.

HELENA

I pray you, though you mock me, gentlemen,
Let her not hurt me: I was never curst;
310 I have no gift at all in shrewishness;
I am a right maid for my cowardice:
Let her not strike me. You perhaps may think,
Because she is something lower than myself,
That I can match her.

*[**Helena** speaks to **Lysander** and **Demetrius**] Gentlemen, I beg of you, even though you'll tease me for it, to not just stand by and let her hurt me. I was never a bitch. I'm just a timid girl. But maybe you think I can handle her because she's shorter than I am.*

HERMIA

315   Lower! hark, again.

Shorter! Ha! There she goes again!

HELENA

Good Hermia, do not be so bitter with me.
I evermore did love you, Hermia,
Did ever keep your counsels, never wrong'd you;
Save that, in love unto Demetrius,
320   I told him of your stealth unto this wood.
He follow'd you; for love I follow'd him;
But he hath chid me hence and threaten'd me
To strike me, spurn me, nay, to kill me too:
And now, so you will let me quiet go,
325   To Athens will I bear my folly back
And follow you no further: let me go:
You see how simple and how fond I am.

*My dear Hermia, don't be so angry with me. I've always loved you, and kept your
secrets, and never did anything wrong to you—except that I told Demetrius about
your plans to run away to the forest tonight, because I was so in love with him. He
followed you, and because I was in love, I followed him. But then he scolded me and
told me to go away. He threatened to hit me, push me aside, even kill me. Now just
let me go quietly back to Athens and take my foolishness with me. I won't follow you
anymore. Just let me go. You see how silly I've been.*

HERMIA

Why, get you gone: who is't that hinders you?

Then go. What's keeping you?

HELENA

A foolish heart, that I leave here behind.

It's my foolish heart that keeps me here.

HERMIA

330   What, with Lysander?

You mean with Lysander?

HELENA

With Demetrius.

No, with Demetrius.

LYSANDER

Be not afraid; she shall not harm thee, Helena.

Helena, don't be afraid. She won't hurt you.

DEMETRIUS

No, sir, she shall not, though you take her part.

No, sir, she won't, not even if you help her.

HELENA

O, when she's angry, she is keen and shrewd!
335   She was a vixen when she went to school;
And though she be but little, she is fierce.

Oh, she's clever and sharp when she's angry. She was sly as a fox when we were in school, and even though she's little, she is fierce.

HERMIA

"Little" again! nothing but "low" and "little"!
Why will you suffer her to flout me thus?
Let me come to her.

*[**Hermia** speaks to **Lysander**] "Little" again! Nothing but "short" and "little"! Why are you letting her insult me like this? Let me at her.*

LYSANDER

340   Get you gone, you dwarf;
        You minimus, of hindering knot-grass made;
        You bead, you acorn.

        Get out of here, you dwarf. You tiny weed-creature! You dot! You acorn!

---

minimus, of hindering knot-grass made: Lysander is calling Hermia a small creature fed on knotgrass, a weed that was believed to stunt the growth of children and animals.

DEMETRIUS

        You are too officious
        In her behalf that scorns your services.
345   Let her alone: speak not of Helena;
        Take not her part; for, if thou dost intend
        Never so little show of love to her,
        Thou shalt aby it.

        [Demetrius speaks to Lysander] You're working awfully hard to protect someone who wants nothing to do with you. Leave Helena alone. Don't say her name or take her side. And if you continue to treat Hermia so badly, you're going to pay for it.

LYSANDER

        Now she holds me not;
350   Now follow, if thou darest, to try whose right,
        Of thine or mine, is most in Helena.

        Hermia has no more hold over me. So come with me, if you dare, and find out who has the right to Helena, you or me.

DEMETRIUS

        Follow! nay, I'll go with thee, cheek by jole.

        Follow you? Certainly not. We'll go side by side.

jole: This is slang for **Jowl**, as in the expression "cheek by jowl," which means "side by side." There's no way that Demetrius is going to walk behind Lysander, like a servant—that would be demeaning.

[Exeunt **Lysander** and **Demetrius**]

[Lysander and Demetrius leave the scene]

HERMIA

You, mistress, all this coil is 'long of you:
Nay, go not back.

You, miss—all this trouble is because of you. Stay right where you are.

HELENA

355   I will not trust you, I,
Nor longer stay in your curst company.
Your hands than mine are quicker for a fray,
My legs are longer though, to run away.

I don't trust you. I won't stay any longer in your bad company. You have quicker hands for a fight, but I have longer legs for running away.

[Exit]
[Helena leaves the scene]

HERMIA

I am amazed, and know not what to say.

I am stunned and don't know what to say.

[Exit]
[Hermia leaves the scene]

OBERON

360   This is thy negligence: still thou mistakest,
Or else committ'st thy knaveries wilfully.

[Oberon speaks to Puck] This is all your fault. Either you're still making mistakes or you're playing tricks on purpose.

PUCK

>Believe me, king of shadows, I mistook.
>Did not you tell me I should know the man
>By the Athenian garment he had on?
365 And so far blameless proves my enterprise,
>That I have 'nointed an Athenian's eyes;
>And so far am I glad it so did sort
>As this their jangling I esteem a sport.

Believe me, it was a mistake. Didn't you tell me that I would recognize the man by his Athenian clothes? You can't blame me for what I did. I put the love juice on an Athenian's eyes, and actually I'm glad I did, because all this fighting is very entertaining.

OBERON

>Thou see'st these lovers seek a place to fight:
370 Hie therefore, Robin, overcast the night;
>The starry welkin cover thou anon
>With drooping fog as black as Acheron,
>And lead these testy rivals so astray
>As one come not within another's way.
375 Like to Lysander sometime frame thy tongue,
>Then stir Demetrius up with bitter wrong;
>And sometime rail thou like Demetrius;
>And from each other look thou lead them thus,
>Till o'er their brows death-counterfeiting sleep
380 With leaden legs and batty wings doth creep:
>Then crush this herb into Lysander's eye;
>Whose liquor hath this virtuous property,
>To take from thence all error with his might,
>And make his eyeballs roll with wonted sight.
385 When they next wake, all this derision
>Shall seem a dream and fruitless vision,
>And back to Athens shall the lovers wend,
>With league whose date till death shall never end.
>Whiles I in this affair do thee employ,

390   I'll to my queen and beg her Indian boy;
       And then I will her charmed eye release
       From monster's view, and all things shall be peace.

Go find these lovers a place to fight. Hurry there, Robin, and make the night darker. Cover the starry sky with a fog as dark as hell, and get these enemies so lost that they won't be in each other's way. Speak in Lysander's voice, and make Demetrius angry by insulting him. Then speak in Demetrius's voice, and say things that will make Lysander mad. Use your voice to chase them away from each other until they're so exhausted they fall asleep. Then put the juice from this flower on Lysander's eyes. This flower has the power to remove the spell of the other flower and will make him see normally again. When they wake up, all this foolishness will seem like a dream and will have had no effect on them. Then the lovers will go back to Athens, bound together by love until their death do them part. While you're busy with this, I'll go back to Titania and ask her for that changeling Indian boy. Then I'll remove the spell from her eyes so she won't be in love with that monster, and everything will be all right again.

welkin: This was a word for the sky or the heavens.

Acheron: This is the name of a river in Hades, as hell is called in Greek mythology.

from each other look thou lead them: Oberon instructs Puck to pull Lysander and Demetrius in different directions by imitating their voices in the dark forest.

crush this herb into Lysander's eye: Here, "herb" means "flower." Oberon has already mentioned this second flower, whose juice undoes the spell of the first one.

PUCK

       My fairy lord, this must be done with haste,
       For night's swift dragons cut the clouds full fast,
395   And yonder shines Aurora's harbinger,
       At whose approach, ghosts, wandering here and there,
       Troop home to churchyards: damned spirits all,
       That in crossways and floods have burial,
       Already to their wormy beds are gone;

400 For fear lest day should look their shames upon,
They willfully themselves exile from light
And must for aye consort with black-brow'd night.

My lord, lord of the fairies, this must be done quickly because night is fading and the morning star is beginning to shine. When she appears, the ghosts go back to the graveyards, and the spirits of suicides return to the crossroads and rivers so they can shun the light and avoid being revealed in all their shame. That's why they come out only at night.

Aurora: This is the name of the morning star. The chariot of the goddess of night was pulled by dragons.

damned spirits all: People who committed suicide were supposed to be buried at crossroads. Puck is also referring to those who have drowned themselves, and whose bodies have never been found. Because suicide was considered shameful, Puck says that the spirits of suicides seek the shadows so they won't risk having their shame exposed to the harsh light of day.

OBERON

But we are spirits of another sort:
I with the morning's love have oft made sport,
405 And, like a forester, the groves may tread,
Even till the eastern gate, all fiery-red,
Opening on Neptune with fair blessed beams,
Turns into yellow gold his salt green streams.
But, notwithstanding, haste; make no delay:
410 We may effect this business yet ere day.

But we are spirits of a different kind. I've often amused myself with the morning's love, and, like the keeper of a forest, I often wander through the woods until the fiery sun rises in the east and shines on the ocean, turning the salty waves yellow gold. But never mind that. Hurry, don't delay. We can finish this business up before daylight.

I with the morning's love have oft made sport: This may be a double entendre, or even a triple entendre. It may be a reference to Cephalon, a hunter who was the lover of Aurora, the goddess of the dawn. In that case, it may mean that Oberon has spent time hunting with Cephalon. Or if "morning's love" is taken to mean love granted by the morning, then it may mean that Oberon has played around with Aurora himself. Other possible meanings of making sport with the morning's love also suggest themselves.

[Exit **Oberon**]
*[**Oberon** leaves the scene]*

PUCK

Up and down, up and down,
I will lead them up and down:
I am fear'd in field and town:
Goblin, lead them up and down.
415   Here comes one.

Up and down, up and down, I will lead them up and down. I'm feared in the country and I'm feared in town. Goblin, lead them up and down. Here comes one of them now.

Goblin: Puck was sometimes also called *Hobgoblin* or *Goblin*.

[Re-enter **Lysander**]
*[**Lysander** reenters the scene]*

LYSANDER

Where art thou, proud Demetrius? speak thou now.

Where are you, Demetrius, you stuck-up jerk? Speak up!

PUCK

Here, villain; drawn and ready. Where art thou?

*[**Puck** speaks in the voice of **Demetrius**] I'm over here, you villain, with my sword drawn, ready to fight. Where are you?*

LYSANDER

I will be with thee straight.

I'll be right there.

PUCK

> Follow me, then,
>
> 420 To plainer ground.

> *[**Puck** continues to speak in the voice of **Demetrius**] Follow me to level ground, where we can fight better.*

[Exit **Lysander**, as following the voice]

*[**Lysander** leaves the scene, in the direction from which the voice is coming]*

[Re-enter **Demetrius**]

*[**Demetrius** reenters the scene]*

DEMETRIUS

> Lysander! Speak again.
>
> Thou runaway, thou coward, art thou fled?
>
> Speak! In some bush? Where dost thou hide thy head?

> *Lysander! Say something. You runaway! You coward! Have you taken off? Speak up! Are you in some bush? Where are you hiding?*

PUCK

> Thou coward, art thou bragging to the stars,
>
> 425 Telling the bushes that thou look'st for wars,
>
> And wilt not come? Come, recreant; come, thou child;
>
> I'll whip thee with a rod: he is defiled
>
> That draws a sword on thee.

> *[**Puck** speaks in the voice of **Lysander**] You coward! You're bragging to high heaven and telling the bushes you're looking for a fight, but why won't you come out? Come on, coward! Come on, punk. I'll beat you with a stick. Anyone would be embarrassed to use a good sword on someone like you.*

---

recreant: This word meant "coward."

he is defiled that draws a sword on thee: Puck, speaking as Lysander, means that he'll beat Demetrius with a stick because it would be a disgrace to use a noble sword on such a coward.

DEMETRIUS

Yea, art thou there?

Hey, are you there?

PUCK

430 Follow my voice: we'll try no manhood here.

*[**Puck** continues to speak in the voice of **Lysander**] Follow me. This place is no good for a fight.*

[Exeunt]
*[**Puck**, **Demetrius**, and **Lysander** leave the scene]*

[Re-enter **Lysander**]
*[**Lysander** reenters the scene]*

LYSANDER

He goes before me and still dares me on:
When I come where he calls, then he is gone.
The villain is much lighter-heel'd than I:
I follow'd fast, but faster he did fly;
435 That fallen am I in dark uneven way,
And here will rest me.
[Lies down]
Come, thou gentle day!
For if but once thou show me thy grey light,
I'll find Demetrius and revenge this spite.

*He runs away from me and still dares me to fight. When I go where I hear his voice, he's gone. That villain is faster than I am. I am fast to follow, but he's faster to run away. Now I'm lost here in the dark and will lie down to rest. [**Lysander** lies down] Come, morning—as soon as I see the first light of dawn, I'll find Demetrius and get revenge on him for these tricks.*

[Sleeps]
*[**Lysander** falls asleep]*

[Re-enter **Puck** and **Demetrius**]
*[**Puck** and **Demetrius** reenter the scene]*

PUCK

440   Ho, ho, ho! Coward, why comest thou not?

*[**Puck** speaks in the voice of **Lysander**] Ha, ha, ha! Aren't you coming, you coward?*

DEMETRIUS

Abide me, if thou darest; for well I wot
Thou runn'st before me, shifting every place,
And darest not stand, nor look me in the face.
Where art thou now?

Wait for me, if you dare. I know you're running around ahead of me, jumping from place to place, not daring to stand or look me in the face. Where are you now?

PUCK

445   Come hither: I am here.

*[**Puck** continues to speak in the voice of **Lysander**] Come this way. I'm here.*

DEMETRIUS

Nay, then, thou mock'st me. Thou shalt buy this dear,
If ever I thy face by daylight see:
Now, go thy way. Faintness constraineth me
To measure out my length on this cold bed.
450   By day's approach look to be visited.

No, you're making fun of me. If I ever see your face in daylight, I'll really make you pay. Now be on your way. Exhaustion forces me to lie down here on the cold ground to get some sleep. Expect to see me in the morning.

[Lies down and sleeps]
*[**Demetrius** lies down and falls asleep]*

[Re-enter **Helena**]
*[**Helena** reenters the scene]*

HELENA

O weary night, O long and tedious night,
Abate thy hour! Shine comforts from the east,

That I may back to Athens by daylight,
From these that my poor company detest:
455 And sleep, that sometimes shuts up sorrow's eye,
Steal me awhile from mine own company.

Oh, exhausting night! Oh, long and tedious night! Make your hours shorter! Let dawn's light comfort me so I can find my way back to Athens in the morning, away from these people who hate me so much. And now, sleep—sleep, which sometimes helps people forget their sorrows—come, sleep, and help me leave myself and my troubles.

[Lies down and sleeps]
*[**Helena** lies down and sleeps]*

PUCK

Yet but three? Come one more;
Two of both kinds make up four.
Here she comes, curst and sad:
460 Cupid is a knavish lad,
Thus to make poor females mad.

Just three of you? Come on, number four. Two of each kind, that makes four. And here she is, bad-tempered and sad. That Cupid is a tricky boy, making these poor girls crazy.

[Re-enter **Hermia**]
*[**Hermia** reenters the scene]*

HERMIA

Never so weary, never so in woe,
Bedabbled with the dew and torn with briers,
I can no further crawl, no further go;
465 My legs can keep no pace with my desires.
Here will I rest me till the break of day.
Heavens shield Lysander, if they mean a fray!

I've never been so tired or so heartbroken, drenched in dew and scraped up by thorns. I can't go on. My legs can't keep up, no matter how much I want to keep going. I'll rest here until dawn. Heaven protect Lysander, if he and Demetrius get into a fight!

[Lies down and sleeps]

[**Hermia** lies down and falls asleep]

PUCK

On the ground
Sleep sound:
470   I'll apply
To your eye,
Gentle lover, remedy.
[Squeezing the juice on Lysander's eyes]
When thou wakest,
Thou takest
475   True delight
In the sight
Of thy former lady's eye:
And the country proverb known,
That every man should take his own,
480   In your waking shall be shown:
Jack shall have Jill;
Nought shall go ill;
The man shall have his mare again, and all shall be well.

[**Puck** speaks to **Lysander**] On the ground, sleeping sound, I'll put this remedy on your eyes, gentle lover. [**Puck** squeezes the juice from the second flower onto **Lysander**'s eyes] When you wake up and see your former lover, you'll be happily back in love with her. As the country saying goes, every man will have his own. When you all wake up, you'll show how every Jack has his Jill, and nothing can go wrong. The man will have his pretty mount again, and all will be well.

[Exit]

[**Puck** leaves the scene]

The act and the scene end here, but the four lovers remain onstage, sleeping.

Act 4

Act 4 Summary

Act 3 ended with Titania enamored of Bottom (who has been halfway transformed into an ass), with the four young Athenian lovers asleep in the forest, and with Puck hoping that he had corrected his earlier mistake by using a different magic flower to make Lysander fall out of love with Helena and back in love with Hermia.

Act 4 provides the resolution of the play. It ties up all the conflicts—by the end of the act, everyone is in love with the person he or she should love, and the Mechanicals are reunited and ready for their play.

The act opens with Titania and her fairies fawning over Bottom, who still has no idea that he has an ass's head, and with Oberon lurking in the background. Titania and Bottom take a nap. Puck comes along, and Oberon explains to him that he has already persuaded Titania to give up the changeling boy in her care, and so the love spell is lifted from Titania. When Titania wakes up, she tells Oberon that she has had a dream about being in love with a monster. Oberon points to Bottom, still asleep, and shows her that she was indeed in love with a monster. Titania is grateful that the spell has been lifted, and she and Oberon go off together while Puck, on Oberon's orders, removes the ass's head from the sleeping Bottom.

Theseus, Hippolyta, and Egeus arrive in the forest to go hunting on the morning of the wedding. But what they find in the forest instead of game is the four young Athenian lovers, asleep. They all wake up and have only vague memories of the strange dream that seems to have brought them here. Hermia and Lysander admit they were running away, which Egeus thinks is reason enough to have Lysander arrested. But Demetrius admits that he's now in love with Helena, and that he was in fact engaged to Helena before he pursued Hermia. Theseus decides that no one should be punished, and that the two couples, now happy, should be married along with himself and Hippolyta. They all return to Athens to prepare for the weddings.

Bottom wakes up with only vague memories of his fantastic dream. But he's none the worse for wear, and he goes off to find the rest of the Mechanicals. They are sad about having lost Bottom as a cast member, and they're ready to call it quits. But Bottom arrives and triumphantly tells them to prepare to perform in front of Theseus and Hippolyta.

Act 4, Scene 1

The same part of the wood

[**Lysander**, **Demetrius**, **Helena**, and **Hermia** lying asleep; enter **Titania** and
Bottom; **Peaseblossom**, **Cobweb**, **Moth**, **Mustardseed**, and other **Fairies**
attending; **Oberon** behind them unseen]

*[**Lysander**, **Demetrius**, **Helena**, and **Hermia** are lying asleep, with **Peaseblossom**,
Cobweb, **Moth**, **Mustardseed**, and other **Fairies** already present, and **Oberon** hidden
behind them, when **Titania** and **Bottom** enter the scene]*

TITANIA

1   Come, sit thee down upon this flowery bed,
    While I thy amiable cheeks do coy,
    And stick musk-roses in thy sleek smooth head,
    And kiss thy fair large ears, my gentle joy.

*Come, sit down upon this bed of flowers. I'll stroke your lovely cheeks and place
roses on your smooth head and kiss those beautiful large ears of yours, my
gentle joy.*

BOTTOM

5   Where's Peaseblossom?

Where's Peaseblossom?

PEASEBLOSSOM

Ready.

Ready.

BOTTOM

Scratch my head, Peaseblossom. Where's Mounsieur Cobweb?

Scratch my head, Peaseblossom. Where's Monsieur Cobweb?

Mounsieur Cobweb: Bottom thinks he's being aristocratic by addressing Cobweb with the French *mounsieur* (or, in modern French, *monsieur*) for "mister."

COBWEB

Ready.

Ready.

BOTTOM

Mounsieur Cobweb, good mounsieur, get you your
10   weapons in your hand, and kill me a red-hipped
humble-bee on the top of a thistle; and, good
mounsieur, bring me the honey-bag. Do not fret
yourself too much in the action, mounsieur; and,
good mounsieur, have a care the honey-bag break not;
15   I would be loath to have you overflown with a
honey-bag, signior. Where's Mounsieur Mustardseed?

Monsieur Cobweb, good monsieur, grab your weapons and find a red-striped bumblebee that's sitting on a thistle. Kill it, and bring me the honey bag. Do not tire yourself out too much while doing this, monsieur—and, good monsieur, be careful not to break the honey bag. I'd be sorry to see you drowned in honey, signor. Where's Mounsieur Mustardseed?

---

signior: Now Bottom shows off by switching to the Italian word for "sir."

MUSTARDSEED

Ready.

Ready.

BOTTOM

Give me your neaf, Mounsieur Mustardseed. Pray you,
leave your courtesy, good mounsieur.

Give me your fist, Monsieur Mustardseed. And, please, sir, don't stand on ceremony—no more bowing, if you please.

MUSTARDSEED

20   What's your Will?

What would you like me to do?

BOTTOM

Nothing, good mounsieur, but to help Cavalery Cobweb
to scratch. I must to the barber's, mounsieur; for
methinks I am marvellous hairy about the face; and I
am such a tender ass, if my hair do but tickle me,

25   I must scratch.

Just help Cavalry Cobweb scratch me, good monsieur. I must go to the barber,
monsieur. My face feels incredibly hairy, and I am such a delicate fool that if my hair
tickles me, I just have to scratch.

Cavalery Cobweb: Here, when Bottom says "cavalery," he means "cavalier,"
which is a grand, courtly gentleman. Note also that earlier Bottom asked to be
scratched by Peaseblossom, not Cobweb, who has been sent to kill the honey-
bee. It's unclear whether this is a transcription error that has persisted over the
centuries or whether Shakespeare purposely wanted to have Bottom make that
mistake. The director of a production of **A Midsummer Night's Dream** can choose
to change the name to Peaseblossom, just leave it as it is, or have fun showing
Cobweb becoming confused.

marvellous hairy about the face: This is another example of dramatic irony.
Bottom notices that his face feels hairy, but he has no idea why. The audience
does, though, and so Bottom's line is even funnier when he calls himself "such
a tender ass."

TITANIA

What, wilt thou hear some music,
my sweet love?

Would you like to hear some music, my sweet love?

BOTTOM

I have a reasonable good ear in music. Let's have
the tongs and the bones.

I have a pretty good ear for music. Let's hear some tongs and bones.

---

the tongs and the bones: Tongs and bones were homemade musical instruments. Tongs were struck, like a triangle, and bones were held in the hand and used to make rattling sounds. These instruments would have been found in a country band—something like an old-fashioned jug band, with one person playing a saw and others playing a washboard, washtub bass, spoons, and so forth. These definitely weren't instruments that fairies would play.

TITANIA

30 Or say, sweet love, what thou desirest to eat.

Or tell me, sweet love, what you feel like eating.

BOTTOM

Truly, a peck of provender: I could munch your good
dry oats. Methinks I have a great desire to a bottle
of hay: good hay, sweet hay, hath no fellow.

I certainly could go for a snack. I could munch on some oats. Actually, I really feel like having a nice bundle of hay. There's nothing like some good sweet hay.

TITANIA

I have a venturous fairy that shall seek
35 The squirrel's hoard, and fetch thee new nuts.

I have a brave fairy who will go and find a squirrel's stash and bring you some fresh nuts.

BOTTOM

I had rather have a handful or two of dried peas.
But, I pray you, let none of your people stir me: I
have an exposition of sleep come upon me.

I'd rather have a handful or two of dried peas. But please don't let any of your people disturb me. I feel a nap coming on.

---
exposition: Here, Bottom means *disposition*, or an inclination to sleep.

TITANIA

Sleep thou, and I will wind thee in my arms.

40 Fairies, begone, and be all ways away.

Go to sleep, and I will wrap you in my arms. Scatter, fairies—make yourselves scarce.

[Exeunt **Fairies**.]
*[All the **Fairies** leave the scene]*

So doth the woodbine the sweet honeysuckle
Gently entwist; the female ivy so
Enrings the barky fingers of the elm.
O, how I love thee! how I dote on thee!

Just like the woodbine, gently entwined with the honeysuckle, and like the female ivy, who wraps herself around the branches of the elm tree, I love you—oh, how I cherish you!

---
the female ivy: Titania is saying that she needs the support of her lover, the man with the ass's head, in the same way that the ivy, a weak vine, needs the support of the great tree.

[They sleep.]
*[**Titania** and **Bottom** fall asleep]*

[Enter **Puck**; **Oberon** advances]
*[**Puck** enters the scene, and **Oberon** steps forward]*

OBERON

45 Welcome, good Robin. See'st thou this sweet sight?
Her dotage now I do begin to pity:
For, meeting her of late behind the wood

Seeking sweet favours from this hateful fool,
I did upbraid her and fall out with her;
50   For she his hairy temples then had rounded
With a coronet of fresh and fragrant flowers;
And that same dew, which sometime on the buds
Was wont to swell like round and orient pearls,
Stood now within the pretty flowerets' eyes
55   Like tears that did their own disgrace bewail.
When I had at my pleasure taunted her
And she in mild terms begg'd my patience,
I then did ask of her her changeling child;
Which straight she gave me, and her fairy sent
60   To bear him to my bower in fairy land.
And now I have the boy, I will undo
This hateful imperfection of her eyes:
And, gentle Puck, take this transformed scalp
From off the head of this Athenian swain;
65   That, he awaking when the other do,
May all to Athens back again repair
And think no more of this night's accident
But as the fierce vexation of a dream.
But first I will release the fairy queen.
[Touching her eyes with an herb]
70   Be as thou wast wont to be;
See as thou wast wont to see:
Dian's bud o'er Cupid's flower
Hath such force and blessed power.
Now, my Titania; wake you, my sweet queen.

Welcome, Robin. Do you see this sweet picture? I'm beginning to feel sorry for her and her foolish love. I just saw her at the edge of the forest, looking for flowers for this horrid fool. I scolded her, and we had a fight. She had put a crown of beautiful flowers on his head. The pearly drops of dew resting on the center of the flowers made it look as though the flowers were crying tears of humiliation for being asked to decorate the head of such an awful being. When I had teased her enough, and she had sweetly asked me to be patient, I asked her for the changeling boy, and she gave him to me right away. She sent a fairy to bring him to my home, and now that I have the boy, I will free her eyes from this dreadful spell. And, kind Puck, take the ass's head off the head of this Athenian charmer so when he wakes up with

the others, they can all go back to Athens and just remember tonight's trouble-
some events as if they'd happened in a dream. But first let me free the fairy queen.
*[**Oberon** anoints the sleeping **Titania**'s eyes with the juice of a second flower, the*
antidote to the juice of the first flower, and speaks to her] Be as you used to be,
see as you used to see. Diana's bud has much more power and blessed force than
Cupid's flower. Now, my Titania, wake up, my sweet queen.

Athenian swain: A *swain* is a dashing, romantic young lover. Oberon is being
sarcastic.

Dian's bud o'er Cupid's flower: "Dian's bud" is what Oberon calls the second
flower, which lifts the spell of the first ("Cupid's flower"). The second flower may
be the flower of the agnus castus, the so-called chaste tree, which was supposed to preserve chastity. The point is that Diana, the goddess of virginity and
purity, is stronger than Cupid, the childish god of love.

TITANIA

75   My Oberon! what visions have I seen!
         Methought I was enamour'd of an ass.

My Oberon! What dreams I've had! I dreamed I was in love with an ass!

OBERON

There lies your love.

That's your love over there.

TITANIA

How came these things to pass?
O, how mine eyes do loathe his visage now!

What happened? Oh, I can't stand the sight of him now!

Titania falls instantly out of love with Bottom. This passage highlights the theme
of love's inconstancy, and how quickly it can come and go.

OBERON

80 Silence awhile. Robin, take off this head.
Titania, music call; and strike more dead
Than common sleep of all these five the sense.

Quiet for a moment. Robin, take off his ass's head. Titania, call for music, and make these five sleep more deeply than the dead.

---

these five: Oberon means Bottom and the four young Athenians.

TITANIA

Music, ho! music, such as charmeth sleep!

Music! Play the sort of music that makes people sleepy!

[Music]
[Music plays]

PUCK

Now, when thou wakest, with thine
85 own fool's eyes peep.

[**Puck** removes the ass's head from **Bottom**]

Now, when you wake up, look with your own foolish eyes.

OBERON

Sound, music! Come, my queen, take hands with me,
And rock the ground whereon these sleepers be.
Now thou and I are new in amity,
And will to-morrow midnight solemnly
90 Dance in Duke Theseus' house triumphantly,
And bless it to all fair prosperity:
There shall the pairs of faithful lovers be
Wedded, with Theseus, all in jollity.

Play, music! Come, my queen, take my hand, and let's dance on the ground where these lovers are sleeping. Now that you and I are friends again, we'll dance happily in the house of Duke Theseus and bless his house with good fortune. These pairs of lovers will be married there, too, along with Theseus and Hippolyta, and share in their celebration.

PUCK

Fairy king, attend, and mark:
95   I do hear the morning lark.

Fairy king, wait and listen. I hear the morning lark.

OBERON

Then, my queen, in silence sad,
Trip we after the night's shade:
We the globe can compass soon,
Swifter than the wandering moon.

Then, my queen, in sad silence let us chase after night's shadows. We can circle the world faster than the moon.

TITANIA

100   Come, my lord, and in our flight
Tell me how it came this night
That I sleeping here was found
With these mortals on the ground.

Come on, my lord, and while we're flying, tell me how I ended up here, sleeping on the ground with these human beings.

[Exeunt **Oberon**, **Titania**, and **Robin**]
*[**Oberon**, **Titania**, and **Puck** leave the scene]*

[Horns winded within]
[Hunting horns are heard offstage]

[Enter **Theseus**, **Hippolyta**, **Egeus**, and **Train**]
*[**Theseus**, **Hippolyta**, **Egeus**, and their **Attendants** enter the scene]*

THESEUS

Go, one of you, find out the forester;
105   For now our observation is perform'd;

And since we have the vaward of the day,
My love shall hear the music of my hounds.
Uncouple in the western valley; let them go:
Dispatch, I say, and find the forester.

*[**Theseus** speaks to his **Attendants**] Go, one of you, and find the groundskeeper. We've performed our May Day rites, and since we have the early part of the day free, my love can listen to my hunting dogs bark as they run unleashed after their prey in the western valley. Turn them loose! Hurry up, now, and find the groundskeeper.*

---

forester: This was the manager, or groundskeeper, of a royal forest or of the forest on a nobleman's estate. The forester would have managed the hunting dogs, bringing them out when his royal or noble employer wanted to hunt.

our observation is perform'd: May Day rites varied from country to country but typically included things like gathering flowers for the day's celebrations and having women wash their faces in the morning dew to keep their complexions beautiful.

vaward: This term means "early morning."

[Exit an **Attendant**]
*[One of the **Attendants** leaves the scene]*

110 We will, fair queen, up to the mountain's top,
And mark the musical confusion
Of hounds and echo in conjunction.

Fair queen, we'll go up to the mountaintop and listen to the musical sound of the hounds barking and howling during the chase.

HIPPOLYTA

I was with Hercules and Cadmus once,
When in a wood of Crete they bay'd the bear
115 With hounds of Sparta: never did I hear
Such gallant chiding: for, besides the groves,
The skies, the fountains, every region near
Seem'd all one mutual cry: I never heard
So musical a discord, such sweet thunder.

One time when I was with Hercules and Cadmus in the woods on the island of Crete,
they chased a bear with hounds from Sparta. I've never heard such valiant bark-
ing—the forest, the skies, the streams, and everywhere nearby seemed to be filled
with a single cry. Never had I heard such a beautiful, musical racket.

> **Hercules and Cadmus:** Hercules is the legendary strongman of Greek mythology,
> and Cadmus is the Phoenician prince who was said to have founded the city of
> Thebes. Hippolyta, as queen of the Amazons, would have known people like them.
>
> **hounds of Sparta:** Spartan hounds were thought to have had extraordinary
> hunting ability.

THESEUS

120 My hounds are bred out of the Spartan kind,
     So flew'd, so sanded, and their heads are hung
     With ears that sweep away the morning dew;
     Crook-knee'd, and dew-lapp'd like Thessalian bulls;
     Slow in pursuit, but match'd in mouth like bells,
125 Each under each. A cry more tuneable
     Was never holla'd to, nor cheer'd with horn,
     In Crete, in Sparta, nor in Thessaly:
     Judge when you hear. But, soft! what nymphs are these?

My hounds are Spartan hounds, with that breed's big jowls, sandy color, and long
ears that sweep away the morning dew. They are bowlegged, with that big flap of skin
at their throats, like Thessalian bulls. They run slowly, but their voices ring out like
bells. In all of Crete, Sparta, and Thessaly, never has a more melodious pack of dogs
*been urged on with voices and horns. Judge for yourself when you hear them. [**The-***
***seus** spots the four sleeping lovers] But wait—who are these beautiful young people?*

> The dogs described in this passage are probably closest to the
> modern-day bloodhound.

EGEUS

     My lord, this is my daughter here asleep;
130 And this, Lysander; this Demetrius is;

This Helena, old Nedar's Helena:
I wonder of their being here together.

My lord, that's my daughter. That's Lysander, and that's Demetrius, and that's old Nedar's daughter Helena. What are they all doing here together?

THESEUS

No doubt they rose up early to observe
The rite of May, and hearing our intent,
135   Came here in grace our solemnity.
But speak, Egeus; is not this the day
That Hermia should give answer of her choice?

They probably got up early to perform their own May Day rites and then heard that we'd be coming here and came for our ceremony, too. But tell me, Egeus, isn't this the day Hermia was supposed to give you her answer about marrying Demetrius?

EGEUS

It is, my lord.

It is, my lord.

THESEUS

Go, bid the huntsmen wake them with their horns.

*[**Theseus** speaks to his **Attendants**] Go tell the huntsmen to blow their horns and wake them up.*

[Horns and shout within. **Lysander**, **Demetrius**, **Helena**, and **Hermia** wake and start up]
*[Horns and shouting are heard offstage; **Lysander**, **Demetrius**, **Helena**, and **Hermia** awake and leap up]*

140   Good morrow, friends. Saint Valentine is past:
Begin these wood-birds but to couple now?

*[**Theseus** speaks to **Lysander**, **Demetrius**, **Helena**, and **Hermia**] Good morning, friends. Saint Valentine's day has passed. Are you little birds just now pairing up?*

Birds were believed to choose their mates on Valentine's Day.

LYSANDER

Pardon, my lord.

Excuse us, my lord.

THESEUS

I pray you all, stand up.
I know you two are rival enemies:
145   How comes this gentle concord in the world,
That hatred is so far from jealousy,
To sleep by hate, and fear no enmity?

*Please stand up, all of you. [**Theseus** speaks to **Lysander** and **Demetrius**] I know you two are enemies. What kind of peace has come over the world, with hated enemies sleeping fearlessly side by side?*

LYSANDER

My lord, I shall reply amazedly,
Half sleep, half waking: but as yet, I swear,
150   I cannot truly say how I came here
But, as I think,—for truly would I speak,
And now do I bethink me, so it is,—
I came with Hermia hither: our intent
Was to be gone from Athens, where we might,
155   Without the peril of the Athenian law.

My lord, I'm confused. I'm half asleep and half awake, but I honestly don't know how I got here. But now that I think—because I do want to speak truthfully—now that I think about it, this is what I know. I came here with Hermia. We were planning to run away together to a place where we could escape the laws of Athens.

EGEUS

Enough, enough, my lord; you have enough:
I beg the law, the law, upon his head.
They would have stolen away; they would, Demetrius,
Thereby to have defeated you and me,
160   You of your wife and me of my consent,
Of my consent that she should be your wife.

*[**Egeus** speaks to **Theseus**] That's enough right there, my lord! You have enough evidence to throw the book at him. They were planning to run away. [**Egeus** speaks to **Demetrius**] They would have defied our will, Demetrius, taking away your right to make my daughter your wife and my right to give my consent—my consent for you to marry her.*

Egeus, as always, stands for law and order.

DEMETRIUS

My lord, fair Helen told me of their stealth,
Of this their purpose hither to this wood;
And I in fury hither follow'd them,
165   Fair Helena in fancy following me.
But, my good lord, I wot not by what power,—
But by some power it is,—my love to Hermia,
Melted as the snow, seems to me now
As the remembrance of an idle gaud
170   Which in my childhood I did dote upon;
And all the faith, the virtue of my heart,
The object and the pleasure of mine eye,
Is only Helena. To her, my lord,
Was I betroth'd ere I saw Hermia:
175   But, like in sickness, did I loathe this food;
But, as in health, come to my natural taste,
Now I do wish it, love it, long for it,
And will for evermore be true to it.

My lord, beautiful Helena told me of their secret plan to meet in this forest. I angrily chased after them, with lovely Helena following out of her love for me. But somehow—I don't know what power caused it—my love for Hermia melted like the snow and now seems as far away to me as some silly little toy that I adored when I was a child. Now, I swear, the one who has the purity of my heart, who pleases my eyes and makes me happy, is Helena, the one I was engaged to before I met Hermia. Then I lost my love for her, just as when you're sick you can't stand the sight of food. Now I'm healthy again, and my appetite has returned. Now I wish for that love. I love it, long for it, and will be forever faithful to it.

fair Helen: The *a* may have dropped here from Helena's name to accommodate the line's iambic pentameter, or the dropped letter may simply reflect an error in transcription.

Helena in fancy following me: Here, the word *fancy* means "love."

THESEUS

> Fair lovers, you are fortunately met:
> 180   Of this discourse we more will hear anon.
> Egeus, I will overbear your will;
> For in the temple by and by with us
> These couples shall eternally be knit:
> And, for the morning now is something worn,
> 185   Our purposed hunting shall be set aside.
> Away with us to Athens; three and three,
> We'll hold a feast in great solemnity.
> Come, Hippolyta.

Dear lovers, it's lucky that we happened to find you. We'll hear more about this story later on. Egeus, I am overriding your wishes. Later, in the temple, let both of these couples be married along with Hippolyta and me. Now, since the morning is almost gone, let's forget about our hunting plans. Off we go to Athens. Three men and three women—we'll have quite a wedding feast. Come with me, Hippolyta.

Once Theseus decides that he and Hippolyta and the other two happy Athenian couples should all be married on the same day, Oberon and Titania also find themselves in harmony once again.

[Exeunt **Theseus**, **Hippolyta**, **Egeus**, and **Train**]
*[**Theseus**, **Hippolyta**, **Egeus**, and the **Attendants** leave the scene]*

DEMETRIUS

> These things seem small and undistinguishable,
> 190   Like far-off mountains turned into clouds.

All those big things that happened last night seem small now, and hard to make out, like mountains so far away that they look like clouds.

HERMIA

Methinks I see these things with parted eye,
When every thing seems double.

When I try to remember, everything is a blur, as if I had double vision.

HELENA

So methinks:
And I have found Demetrius like a jewel,
195 Mine own, and not mine own.

Me, too—and now I have Demetrius, like a precious jewel I stumbled upon, and even though I have it in my hand, I can hardly believe it belongs to me.

DEMETRIUS

Are you sure
That we are awake? It seems to me
That yet we sleep, we dream. Do not you think
The duke was here, and bid us follow him?

Are you sure we're awake? It feels as if we're still asleep and dreaming. Wasn't the duke here, and didn't he ask us to follow him?

HERMIA

200 Yea; and my father.

Yes, he was here, and so was my father.

HELENA

And Hippolyta.

Hippolyta, too.

LYSANDER

And he did bid us follow to the temple.

And he told us to follow him to the temple.

DEMETRIUS

Why, then, we are awake: let's follow him
And by the way let us recount our dreams.

Well, then, we must be awake. Let's follow him, and on our way we can tell each other what we dreamed.

This passage shows the four young lovers trying to figure out which of their memories are real and which are not, since dreams blur the line between appearances and reality—a major theme of the play.

[Exeunt]
*[**Lysander**, **Demetrius**, **Helena**, and **Hermia** leave the scene]*

BOTTOM

205   [Waking] When my cue comes, call me, and I will
answer: my next is, "Most fair Pyramus." Heigh-ho!
Peter Quince! Flute, the bellows-mender! Snout,
the tinker! Starveling! God's my life, stolen
hence, and left me asleep! I have had a most rare
210   vision. I have had a dream, past the wit of man to
say what dream it was: man is but an ass, if he go
about to expound this dream. Methought I was—there
is no man can tell what. Methought I was,—and
methought I had,—but man is but a patched fool, if
215   he will offer to say what methought I had. The eye
of man hath not heard, the ear of man hath not
seen, man's hand is not able to taste, his tongue
to conceive, nor his heart to report, what my dream
was. I will get Peter Quince to write a ballad of
220   this dream: it shall be called "Bottom's Dream,"
because it hath no bottom; and I will sing it in the
latter end of a play, before the duke:
peradventure, to make it the more gracious, I shall
sing it at her death.

*[**Bottom** wakes up]* When it's my cue, call me, and I will answer. My next cue is, "Most beautiful Pyramus." Whoa! Peter Quince! Flute, the bellows mender! Snout, the tinker! Starveling! I swear on my life, they left me asleep and sneaked away! I have had a most incredible dream, a dream that's almost impossible to describe. Anyone who tried to explain it would sound like an ass. I thought I was—I can hardly say what. I thought I was, and I thought I had . . . well, any man would sound like a fool if he said what I thought I had. No man's eye has heard, no man's ear has seen, no man's hand has tasted, no man's tongue can imagine, and no man's heart has ever described what happened in this dream. I will get Peter Quince to write a ballad about it. It will be called "Bottom's Dream" because it was so deep, it's as if it had no bottom. I will sing it near the end of the play, right in front of the duke. Even better, to make it more elegant, I will sing it right when Thisby dies.

---

past the wit of man: Bottom, like the Athenians, is having trouble figuring out what actually happened and what was a dream.

man is but an ass: Here is more dramatic irony from Bottom, who literally had the head of an ass and now will figuratively make an ass of himself.

patched fool: This term refers to the professional "uniform" of a clown or jester, who wore costumes made from patches of motley, a multicolored woolen fabric of the period.

The eye of man hath not heard: This phrase begins Bottom's mixed-up version of a passage from the Bible: "Eye hath not seen, nor ear heard, neither have entered into the heart of man, the things which God hath prepared for them that love him" (1 Corinthians 2:9).

ballad: This is a type of poem that tells a story.

[Exit]
*[**Bottom** leaves the scene]*

Act 4, Scene 2

Athens, a room in Quince's house

[Enter **Quince**, **Flute**, **Snout**, and **Starveling**]

[Quince, Flute, Snout, and Starveling enter the scene]

QUINCE

1   Have you sent to Bottom's house? Is he come home yet?

Has anybody been to Bottom's house? Is he home yet?

STARVELING

He cannot be heard of. Out of doubt he is
transported.

No one's heard from him. He must have been taken away by the fairies.

FLUTE

If he come not, then the play is marred: it goes
5   not forward, doth it?

If he doesn't come, then the play is ruined. We can't go on, can we?

QUINCE

It is not possible: you have not a man in all
Athens able to discharge Pyramus but he.

No, that wouldn't be possible. Bottom is the only man in Athens who could play Pyramus.

FLUTE

No, he hath simply the best wit of any handicraft
man in Athens.

That's right. He's the funniest tradesman in Athens, hands down.

QUINCE

10 Yea and the best person too; and he is a very
paramour for a sweet voice.

*He is, and he's the best-looking one, too. And he is the very paramour
of a beautiful voice.*

FLUTE

You must say "paragon": a paramour is, God bless us,
a thing of naught.

You mean "paragon." A paramour, God help us, is something bad.

Flute is correct—Quince does indeed mean paragon, or the perfect model of
something, since a paramour is a secret lover.

[Enter **Snug**]
*[**Snug** enters the scene]*

SNUG

Masters, the duke is coming from the temple, and
15 there is two or three lords and ladies more married: if our
sport had gone forward, we had all been made men.

*My friends, the duke is coming back from the temple, with two or three more lords
and ladies who just got married, too. If we had been able to put on our play, we
could have made a fortune.*

FLUTE

O sweet bully Bottom! Thus hath he lost sixpence a
day during his life; he could not have 'scaped
sixpence a day: an the duke had not given him
20 sixpence a day for playing Pyramus, I'll be hanged;
he would have deserved it: sixpence a day in
Pyramus, or nothing.

Good old Bottom! Now he's lost a pension of sixpence a day for the rest of his life. He wouldn't have received less than sixpence a day for playing Pyramus. Hang me if he wouldn't have deserved that. Sixpence a day or nothing at all, I swear.

The mechanicals were under the impression that the duke was going to reward them for their performance.

[Enter **Bottom**]
[***Bottom*** *enters the scene*]

BOTTOM

Where are these lads? Where are these hearts?

Where are you, guys? Where are my good friends?

QUINCE

Bottom! O most courageous day! O most happy hour!

Bottom! It's so great to see you!

BOTTOM

25   Masters, I am to discourse wonders: but ask me not
what; for if I tell you, I am no true Athenian. I
will tell you every thing, right as it fell out.

Guys, I could tell you some amazing things, but don't ask me what, because if I tell you, I'm no Athenian. I will tell you everything, just the way it happened.

Typically, Bottom insists that he absolutely can't tell them what happened, then promises that he'll tell them everything.

QUINCE

Let us hear, sweet Bottom.

Tell us, Bottom.

BOTTOM

Not a word of me. All that I will tell you is, that
30 the duke hath dined. Get your apparel together,
good strings to your beards, new ribbons to your
pumps; meet presently at the palace; every man look
o'er his part; for the short and the long is, our
play is preferred. In any case, let Thisby have
35 clean linen; and let not him that plays the lion
pare his nails, for they shall hang out for the
lion's claws. And, most dear actors, eat no onions
nor garlic, for we are to utter sweet breath; and I
do not doubt but to hear them say, it is a sweet
40 comedy. No more words: away! go, away!

I won't say a word. All I'll tell you is that the duke has had his wedding feast. Get your costumes together, tie on your fake beards, put new ribbons in your shoes, and get ready to meet at the palace. Look over your lines, everybody, because the fact is, our play has been chosen. So let Thisby put on clean underwear, and let whoever is playing the lion not trim his nails, so they'll be long like a lion's claws. And, my dear friends and fellow actors, don't eat any onions or garlic, because we need to have fresh breath—and I'm sure we'll hear them say it's a fresh comedy. No more talking. Go on—get ready!

[Exeunt]
*[All the **Mechanicals** leave the scene]*

Act 5

Act 5 Summary

At the end of act 4, all the play's loose ends were tied up, and all the characters were happily reunited. As act 5 begins, all that remains is to watch the Mechanicals' play—and the sole purpose of act 5 seems to be the fun of this play within the play.

The wedding ceremonies are concluded, and Theseus and Hippolyta are consulting with Philostrate, the master of revels, to select the evening's entertainment from a list of offerings. Theseus and Hippolyta see the description of the Mechanicals' play and decide that it sounds like the most amusing possibility, despite Philostrate's warning that the play is just dreadful. The Mechanicals arrive and perform, and their play is indeed awful, but it's hilariously bad. The Athenians keep up a running commentary of jokes during the performance. The Mechanicals' play within the play ends with a dance, and the Athenian couples head off to enjoy their wedding nights. When everyone has gone, the fairies arrive to bless Theseus's palace as well as the three marriages and the three couples' future children. The play itself ends with an epilogue from Puck, who asks the audience to forgive any missteps and consider any offenses to have been nothing but a dream. He then asks for applause.

Act 5, Scene 1

Athens, the palace of Theseus

[Enter **Theseus, Hyppolyta, Philostrate, Lords** and **Attendants**]

[Theseus, Hyppolyta, Philostrate, Lords, and Attendants enter the scene]

HIPPOLYTA

1   'Tis strange my Theseus, that these
     lovers speak of.

These lovers speak of such strange things, my Theseus.

THESEUS

     More strange than true: I never may believe
     These antique fables, nor these fairy toys.
5   Lovers and madmen have such seething brains,
     Such shaping fantasies, that apprehend
     More than cool reason ever comprehends.
     The lunatic, the lover and the poet
     Are of imagination all compact:
10   One sees more devils than vast hell can hold,
     That is, the madman: the lover, all as frantic,
     Sees Helen's beauty in a brow of Egypt:
     The poet's eye, in fine frenzy rolling,
     Doth glance from heaven to earth, from earth to heaven;
15   And as imagination bodies forth
     The forms of things unknown, the poet's pen
     Turns them to shapes and gives to airy nothing
     A local habitation and a name.
     Such tricks hath strong imagination,
20   That if it would but apprehend some joy
     It comprehends some bringer of that joy;
     Or in the night, imagining some fear,
     How easy is a bush supposed a bear!

Too strange to be true. I never believe those kinds of silly stories and tales about fairies. Lovers and madmen have overheated brains and overactive imaginations that make them see things that cool, reasonable minds could never understand. The madman, the lover, and the poet are formed by their imaginations. The madman sees more devils than hell could ever hold. The lover, just as crazy, sees the beauty of Helen of Troy in the face of a common gypsy. The poet's crazy eyes mix up the earth with heaven, and then his pen writes about unreal things as if they were real. A strong imagination can play such tricks that if it perceives some joy, it will invent some story for that joy. Or if, in the night, it feels some fear, it's very easy to imagine that a bush is a bear.

---

the lunatic, the lover and the poet: Similarity between lovers and lunatics is one of the themes of the play. Shakespeare sees love as strange, unreliable, and like a form of madness. He also pokes fun at himself by grouping poets with the other crazies.

Helen's beauty in a brow of Egypt: "Helen" is Helen of Troy, whose beauty was said to have sparked the Trojan War. The "brow of Egypt" refers to gypsies, seen as darker-skinned, like people from Egypt. As noted in act 3, fair skin was more highly valued than dark skin during this period.

Throughout this speech, Theseus is very clear about what is real and what is not. Notably, he's one of the characters who doesn't venture into the forest at night. Back in Athens, in daylight, the world is clear, and magic doesn't exist, unlike in the forest, where nature lends itself to wildness and magic.

HIPPOLYTA

But all the story of the night told over,
25   And all their minds transfigured so together,
More witnesseth than fancy's images
And grows to something of great constancy;
But, howsoever, strange and admirable.

But they all told the same story as if they had the same mind. This evidence makes it seem as if there is more here than imagination. When everyone repeats the same thing over and over, it begins to seem as if it must be true, no matter how weird it sounds.

Hippolyta doesn't say much during the play, but it's interesting to note that she is the only one who believes the lovers' story.

THESEUS

Here come the lovers, full of joy and mirth.

Here come the lovers, full of happiness and laughter.

[Enter **Lysander**, **Demetrius**, **Hermia**, and **Helena**]
*[**Lysander**, **Demetrius**, **Hermia**, and **Helena** enter the scene]*

30   Joy, gentle friends! Joy and fresh days of love
Accompany your hearts!

I wish you joy, fine friends. May joy and many days of love fill your hearts!

LYSANDER

More than to us
Wait in your royal walks, your board, your bed!

May you find more joy and love ahead in your royal estates, your table, and your bedroom!

THESEUS

Come now; what masques, what dances shall we have,
35   To wear away this long age of three hours
Between our after-supper and bed-time?
Where is our usual manager of mirth?
What revels are in hand? Is there no play,
To ease the anguish of a torturing hour?
40   Call Philostrate.

Come on now, what play, what dancing shall we have to entertain us during the three long hours between our dinner and our bedtime? Where is the manager of our entertainments? What fun does he have planned? Isn't there any amusement to make this agonizing time pass more quickly? Call Philostrate.

Theseus is essentially saying that they are all anxious to have sex with their new spouses and need something to entertain them until it's time for them to go to bed.

PHILOSTRATE

Here, mighty Theseus.

Here I am, mighty Theseus.

THESEUS

Say, what abridgement have you for this evening?
What masque? what music? How shall we beguile
The lazy time, if not with some delight?

Say, what pastime do you have for tonight? What play? What music? How will we pass this time without some kind of entertainment?

abridgement: We think of this word as referring to a shortened form, as in the abridgement of a book. Here, it means "pastime."

PHILOSTRATE

45   There is a brief how many sports are ripe:
Make choice of which your highness will see first.

Here is a list of the entertainments that are ready. Choose the one you would like to see first.

[Giving a paper]
*[**Philostrate** hands **Theseus** a sheet of paper from which **Theseus** reads]*

THESEUS

"The battle with the Centaurs, to be sung
By an Athenian eunuch to the harp."
We'll none of that: that have I told my love,
50   In glory of my kinsman Hercules.
[Reads]

"The riot of the tipsy Bacchanals,
Tearing the Thracian singer in their rage."
That is an old device; and it was play'd
When I from Thebes came last a conqueror.
[Reads]
55   "The thrice three Muses mourning for the death
Of Learning, late deceased in beggary."
That is some satire, keen and critical,
Not sorting with a nuptial ceremony.
[Reads]
"A tedious brief scene of young Pyramus
60   And his love Thisbe; very tragical mirth."
Merry and tragical! tedious and brief!
That is, hot ice and wondrous strange snow.
How shall we find the concord of this discord?

*[**Theseus** reads] "The battle with the Centaurs, as sung by an Athenian eunuch play-ing the harp." Not that one—I already told Hippolyta about that one while telling her stories about my cousin Hercules. [**Theseus** reads] "The riot of the drunk Baccha-nals, in their rage tearing the Thracian singers to pieces." That's an old story. They were doing that one back when I conquered Thebes. [**Theseus** reads] "The three times three Muses mourning the death of knowledge, killed by lack of interest." That's a sharp satire, not really fun for a wedding celebration. [**Theseus** reads] "A tedious brief scene of young Pyramus and his love Thisbe; very tragical mirth." Funny and sad? Long and boring, yet short? This is a mix of hot ice and incredibly strange snow. How shall we bring peace to this disorder?*

---

battle with the Centaurs: This phrase refers to the battle between the Centaurs and the Lapithae during the wedding of Pirithous, a friend of Theseus, when the Centaurs tried to kidnap the bride, Hippodamia. According to some versions of the story, Hercules fought in this battle.

eunuch: The word for a man who was castrated as a boy, sometimes as a way of preserving his boyish soprano voice.

riot of the tipsy Bacchanals: This phrase refers to an occasion on which Orpheus, a musician from Thrace, was torn apart by the Bacchantes, female fol-lowers of Bacchus, the Greek god of wine.

thrice three Muses mourning: The nine Muses are Greek goddesses who were believed to preside over song, poetry, and the arts and sciences. They are Calliope, Muse of epic song; Clio, Muse of history; Euterpe, Muse of lyric song; Thalia, Muse of comedy and bucolic (natural) poetry; Melpomene, Muse of tragedy; Terpsichore, Muse of dance; Erato, Muse of erotic poetry; Polyhymnia, Muse of sacred song; and Urania, Muse of astronomy.

strange snow: It's possible that "strange" is a printing or transcription error, and that there should be a word here that contradicts "snow" the way "hot" does with "ice."

PHILOSTRATE

> A play there is, my lord, some ten words long,
> 65 Which is as brief as I have known a play;
> But by ten words, my lord, it is too long,
> Which makes it tedious; for in all the play
> There is not one word apt, one player fitted:
> And tragical, my noble lord, it is;
> 70 For Pyramus therein doth kill himself.
> Which, when I saw rehearsed, I must confess,
> Made mine eyes water; but more merry tears
> The passion of loud laughter never shed.

My lord, this play is about ten words long, which is the shortest play I've ever seen. But ten words is too long for this play—that's why it is tedious. In the entire play there's not one word said right or one actor suited to his role. It is tragic in a way, though, my noble lord. When Pyramus killed himself, I cried—but from laughing harder than I've ever laughed in my life.

THESEUS

> What are they that do play it?

Who performs this play?

PHILOSTRATE

> 75 Hard-handed men that work in Athens here,
> Which never labour'd in their minds till now,

And now have toil'd their unbreathed memories
With this same play, against your nuptial.

Rough-handed men who work in Athens, who have never used their minds until now, and have now overtaxed their memories in preparing this play for your wedding day.

The hands were said to reveal a person's social class. Tradesmen, or craftsmen who made things with their hands, were associated with rough, callused palms. Smooth, unblemished hands were associated with scholars and others who worked with their minds rather than their hands, and with noblemen, who often didn't work at all.

THESEUS

And we will hear it.

Then we'll see this one.

PHILOSTRATE

80   No, my noble lord;
It is not for you: I have heard it over,
And it is nothing, nothing in the world;
Unless you can find sport in their intents,
Extremely stretch'd and conn'd with cruel pain,
85   To do you service.

No, my noble lord, it's not something you want to see. I have seen it, and it's worth-less—unless you think it would be funny to watch how these men, who are so serious, have strained themselves and put themselves through such pain to learn their few lines.

THESEUS

I will hear that play;
For never anything can be amiss,
When simpleness and duty tender it.
Go, bring them in: and take your places, ladies.

I will watch that play. Nothing's ever that bad when it's done sincerely. Go, bring them in. Please be seated, ladies.

[Exit **Philostrate**]
*[**Philostrate** leaves the scene]*

HIPPOLYTA

90   I love not to see wretchedness o'er charged
And duty in his service perishing.

I don't like to see feeble people embarrass themselves when they're just trying to do something out of loyalty.

THESEUS

Why, gentle sweet, you shall see no such thing.

My darling, you won't see anything like that.

HIPPOLYTA

He says they can do nothing in this kind.

He said they don't know how to put on a play.

THESEUS

The kinder we, to give them thanks for nothing.
95   Our sport shall be to take what they mistake:
And what poor duty cannot do, noble respect
Takes it in might, not merit.
Where I have come, great clerks have purposed
To greet me with premeditated welcomes;
100   Where I have seen them shiver and look pale,
Make periods in the midst of sentences,
Throttle their practised accent in their fears
And in conclusion dumbly have broke off,
Not paying me a welcome. Trust me, sweet,
105   Out of this silence yet I pick'd a welcome;
And in the modesty of fearful duty
I read as much as from the rattling tongue
Of saucy and audacious eloquence.
Love, therefore, and tongue-tied simplicity
110   In least speak most, to my capacity.

Then it will be even kinder of us to thank them when they do poorly. We'll enjoy our-
selves as we note their mistakes and respect them more for how hard they've tried,
with their limited abilities, than for how well they've done. When I've arrived in cities,
I've had famous scholars come to greet me with rehearsed speeches but begin to
tremble, turn pale, and stop in midsentence, forgetting how they planned to say
their words, and then trail off in silence, forgetting to give me the welcome they had
planned. Trust me, darling, out of this silence I have managed to salvage a welcome;
the sincere attempts of a stuttering tongue ring just as true as the words of a loud,
overconfident speaker. Love and hesitating simplicity say the most with the least, in
my opinion.

[Re-enter **Philostrate**]
*[**Philostrate** reenters the scene]*

PHILOSTRATE

So please your grace, the Prologue is address'd.

If it please your grace, here is the Prologue.

THESEUS

Let him approach.

Let him step forward.

The actor who recited the prologue was also called "Prologue."

[Flourish of trumpets]
[A trumpet fanfare is heard]

[Enter **Quince** for the **PROLOGUE**]
*[**Quince** enters the scene as the **PROLOGUE**]*

PROLOGUE

[delivered by **Quince**]
If we offend, it is with our good will.
That you should think, we come not to offend,
115   But with good will. To show our simple skill,
That is the true beginning of our end.
Consider then we come but in despite.

We do not come as minding to contest you,
Our true intent is. All for your delight
120 We are not here. That you should here repent you,
The actors are at hand and by their show
You shall know all that you are like to know.

*[delivered by **Quince**] If we do anything wrong, it is with our best intentions. That you might think. We don't plan to offend, but come with the best intentions. To show our small talents, that is really what we want to do. Consider then that we come in defiance. We don't come intending to battle you, our real intent is. All to entertain you we are not here. That you should here apologize, the actors are ready and they will show you all you need to know.*

Quince's prologue is intended both to announce that the Mechanicals have come to entertain the audience and to apologize in advance if the players should happen to do anything that gives offense. This type of preemptive apology was not uncommon; for example, Shakespeare includes one in the last two lines of the prologue to ***Romeo and Juliet***. But Quince jumbles it up, repeats himself, and punctuates it poorly, so he ends up reading it in an odd, halting manner that doesn't make sense. It's typical of the comedy in this scene—the Mechanicals try to do something that they think is proper for a play, but they mess it up.

THESEUS

This fellow doth not stand upon points.

This guy doesn't pay much attention to details—such as punctuation.

LYSANDER

He hath rid his prologue like a rough colt; he knows
125 not the stop. A good moral, my lord: it is not
enough to speak, but to speak true.

He rode his prologue as if it were an unbroken colt—he doesn't know how to stop. A good lesson, my lord: it's not enough to speak; you must also speak correctly.

---

stop: This means "period," which is to say that Quince doesn't know where to put the periods in his sentences.

HIPPOLYTA

Indeed he hath played on his prologue like a child
on a recorder; a sound, but not in government.

Indeed, he played his prologue the way a child plays a recorder—plenty of sound, but no melody.

THESEUS

His speech, was like a tangled chain; nothing
130   impaired, but all disordered. Who is next?

His speech was like a tangled chain—nothing broken, but all out of order. Who is next?

[Enter **PYRAMUS** and **THISBE, WALL, MOONSHINE,** and **LION**]
[***Bottom*** *enters the scene as* **PYRAMUS** *along with* **Flute** *as* **THISBE**, **Snout** *as* **WALL**, **Starveling** *as* **MOONSHINE**, *and* **Snug** *as* **LION**]

PROLOGUE

Gentles, perchance you wonder at this show;
But wonder on, till truth make all things plain.
This man is Pyramus, if you would know;
This beauteous lady Thisby is certain.
135   This man, with lime and rough-cast, doth present
Wall, that vile Wall which did these lovers sunder;
And through Wall's chink, poor souls, they are content
To whisper. At the which let no man wonder.
This man, with lanthorn, dog, and bush of thorn,
140   Presenteth Moonshine; for, if you will know,
By moonshine did these lovers think no scorn
To meet at Ninus' tomb, there, there to woo.
This grisly beast, which Lion hight by name,
The trusty Thisby, coming first by night,
145   Did scare away, or rather did affright;
And, as she fled, her mantle she did fall,
Which Lion vile with bloody mouth did stain.
Anon comes Pyramus, sweet youth and tall,
And finds his trusty Thisby's mantle slain:

150 Whereat, with blade, with bloody blameful blade,
He bravely broach'd his boiling bloody breast;
And Thisby, tarrying in mulberry shade,
His dagger drew, and died. For all the rest,
Let Lion, Moonshine, Wall, and lovers twain
155 At large discourse, while here they do remain.

Ladies and gentlemen, perhaps you wonder about what will happen in this show. Wonder on, until everything becomes clear. This man is Pyramus, if you'd like to know. This beautiful lady is certainly Thisby. This man, covered in lime and plaster, stands in as Wall, that mean, terrible wall that kept these lovers apart, so they have to settle for whispering to each other through a hole in Wall. No one should wonder who this is—this man with lantern, dog, and thorn bush represents Moonshine, for, if you'd like to know, these lovers didn't think it was any disgrace to meet under Moonshine at Ninus's tomb, there to truly court each other. This horrible beast, Lion by name, saw trustworthy Thisby, who arrived first at the tomb, and scared her, or frightened her, that is, away. As she ran, her cloak fell on the ground. Lion picked it up in his bloody mouth, staining it with blood. Then along comes Pyramus, a tall, handsome young man. When he finds his Thisby's cloak murdered, he takes his bloody, blameful sword and bravely pierces his pounding, bloody heart. Then Thisby, waiting in the mulberry tree's shade, takes Pyramus's sword and kills herself. Now, for the rest of the story, let Lion, Moonshine, Wall, and the lovers tell about it in more detail, while they stay here.

with blade, with bloody blameful blade: Quince thinks he's being quite poetic with all this *b*-based alliteration, but he overuses it, to comic effect.

bravely broach'd his boiling bloody breast: The verb *broach'd* would have been used in connection with penetrating a cask of wine so that its contents could be drawn out. Again, Quince's imagery is more comic than tragic, since a better word here might have been *pierc'd*.

As Quince recites the play's prologue, introducing the characters and giving a synopsis of the plot before turning the stage over to the other actors, they silently act out the events he describes. This type of "dumb show" was common in Elizabethan theater.

[Exeunt **PROLOGUE, THISBE, LION,** and **MOONSHINE**]
[PROLOGUE, THISBE, LION, and MOONSHINE leave the scene]

THESEUS

I wonder if the lion be to speak.

I wonder if the lion is going to speak.

DEMETRIUS

No wonder, my lord: one lion may, when many asses do.

It wouldn't be any wonder, my lord—one lion may indeed speak when so many asses have done so.

Demetrius uses "asses" to mean "idiots."

WALL

[delivered by **Snout**]
In this same interlude it doth befall
That I, one Snout by name, present a wall;
160 And such a wall, as I would have you think,
That had in it a crannied hole or chink,
Through which the lovers, Pyramus and Thisby,
Did whisper often very secretly.
This loam, this rough-cast and this stone doth show
165 That I am that same wall; the truth is so:
And this the cranny is, right and sinister,
Through which the fearful lovers are to whisper.

*[delivered by **Snout**] At this time, as it happens, I, Snout by name, play a wall. And this particular wall, as I'd like you to imagine, had in it a cracked hole, or a chink. Through that chink, the lovers Pyramus and Thisby often whispered secretly. This mud, this plaster, and this stone does show you that I am that very wall, and that is the truth. And this crack, running from right to left, is where the scared lovers are about to whisper.*

---

right and sinister: This word **sinister** meant "left." Its use here is probably intended to rhyme with **whisper**.

THESEUS

Would you desire lime and hair to speak better?

Could plaster possibly speak any better?

DEMETRIUS

It is the wittiest partition that ever I heard
170 discourse, my lord.

That is the cleverest wall I have ever heard speak, my lord.

Throughout the play, Theseus, Hippolyta, and the four newlyweds have fun laughing at how dreadful it is, just the way people laugh at bad movies today.

[Enter **PYRAMUS**]
*[**PYRAMUS** enters the scene]*

THESEUS

Pyramus draws near the wall: silence!

Pyramus is coming to the wall. Quiet!

PYRAMUS

[delivered by **Bottom**]
O grim-look'd night! O night with hue so black!
O night, which ever art when day is not!
O night, O night! alack, alack, alack,
175 I fear my Thisby's promise is forgot!
And thou, O wall, O sweet, O lovely wall,
That stand'st between her father's ground and mine!
Thou wall, O wall, O sweet and lovely wall,
Show me thy chink, to blink through with mine eyne!

*[delivered by **Bottom**] Oh, angry night! Oh, night of such a black color! Oh night, which is always here when day is not! Oh night, oh night! Woe is me! Woe is me! Woe is me! I'm worried my Thisby has forgotten her promise! And you, oh wall—oh sweet, oh lovely wall—that stands between her father's land and mine! You, wall, oh wall, oh sweet and lovely wall, show me your hole so I can look through it with my eye!*

[**WALL** holds up his fingers]

*[**WALL** holds up his fingers]*

180   Thanks, courteous wall: Jove shield thee well for this!
But what see I? No Thisby do I see.
O wicked wall, through whom I see no bliss!
Cursed be thy stones for thus deceiving me!

Thanks, kind wall. May Jupiter protect you for helping us! But what do I see? I don't see Thisby. Oh, wicked wall, I don't see any happiness when I look through you. A curse upon your stones for playing such a trick on me.

THESEUS

The wall, methinks, being sensible, should curse again.

Since the wall is alive, I think it should curse back.

PYRAMUS

185   [**PYRAMUS** addresses **Theseus**] No, in truth, sir, he should not. "Deceiving me" is Thisby's cue: she is to enter now, and I am to spy her through the wall. You shall see, it will fall pat as I told you. Yonder she comes.

*[**PYRAMUS** speaks to **Theseus**] No, actually, he shouldn't. "Playing such a trick on me" is Thisby's cue to enter now, and then I see her through the wall. You'll see, it will all happen, just like I said. Here she comes.*

Bottom doesn't get Theseus's sarcasm. He thinks Theseus is speaking seriously, and so he breaks character to explain what's going on. Since the audience is aware that Theseus is joking, Bottom's reaction is even funnier—and that, of course, is an instance of dramatic irony.

[Enter **THISBE**]

*[**THISBE** enters the scene]*

THISBE

[delivered by **Flute**]
O wall, full often hast thou heard my moans,
190   For parting my fair Pyramus and me!

My cherry lips have often kiss'd thy stones,
Thy stones with lime and hair knit up in thee.

*[delivered by **Flute**] Oh wall, you've heard me cry so often over this separation between my beautiful Pyramus and me! My cherry red lips have often kissed your stones, which are bound together with lime and hair.*

Quince has instructed Flute to play Thisby with a high, girlish voice. The actor playing this part generally uses a falsetto, which can alternate amusingly with his regular voice. In addition, there is definitely some sexually suggestive word-play throughout this scene—any reference to stones can be read as implying the word **testicles**.

PYRAMUS

[delivered by **Bottom**] I see a voice: now will I to the chink,
To spy an I can hear my Thisby's face. Thisby!

*[delivered by **Bottom**] I see a voice—now I'll go back to the hole, to look and see if I can hear my Thisby's face. Thisby!*

Pyramus/Bottom mixes up **see** and **hear**.

THISBE

195 My love thou art, my love I think.

You are my love, or I think you're my love.

PYRAMUS

Think what thou wilt, I am thy lover's grace;
And, like Limander, am I trusty still.

Think what you want, I am your lover. And, like Limander, I can still be trusted.

Limander: Bottom means **Leander**. Hero and Leander are a pair of famous lovers in Greek mythology. As is so often the case with mythical lovers, they both die tragically.

THISBE

And I like Helen, till the Fates me kill.

And I can still be trusted, too, like Helen, until the Fates kill me.

> Thisbe/Flute doesn't mean Helen but Hero, Leander's lover. Hero drowns herself after Leander drowns while swimming across the sea to visit her. Flute's mix-up is amusing, since the most famous Helen—Helen of Troy—is not at all faithful to her husband.

PYRAMUS

Not Shafalus to Procrus was so true.

Not even Shafalus was as faithful to Procrus as I am to you.

> Pyramus/Bottom is trying here for a reference to another mythological pair, Cephalus and Procris. They are a married couple, deeply in love, but each suspects the other of having an affair. Procris spies on Cephalus while he's hunting and is accidentally killed by him.

THISBE

200   As Shafalus to Procrus, I to you.

And I'm faithful to you, too, as Shafalus was to Procrus.

> It's ironic that these examples of faithfulness involve two people who both feared betrayal by the other. Elizabethan audiences would have understood the joke, since they were quite familiar with these mythological stories.

PYRAMUS

O kiss me through the hole of this vile wall!

Oh, kiss me through the hole of this horrible wall!

THISBE

I kiss the wall's hole, not your lips at all.

I'm kissing the wall's hole, not your lips at all.

Just as **stones** can be sexual wordplay, so can **hole**. Pyramus/Bottom and
Thisbe/Flute aren't getting the joke, which is clearly for the entertainment of
the groundlings.

PYRAMUS

Wilt thou at Ninny's tomb meet me straightway?

Will you meet me at Ninny's tomb right away?

THISBE

'Tide life, 'tide death, I come without delay.

Come life, come death, I come without delay.

[Exeunt **PYRAMUS** and **THISBE**]
[PYRAMUS and THISBE leave the scene]

WALL

205   Thus have I, Wall, my part discharged so;
And, being done, thus Wall away doth go.

Now I, Wall, have finished my part, and since I'm done, I'll go away.

[Exit]
[WALL leaves the scene]

THESEUS

Now is the mural down between the two neighbours.

Now the wall is down between the two neighbors

DEMETRIUS

No remedy, my lord, when walls are so wilful to hear
without warning.

What can you do, my lord, when walls are so willing to listen in on things?

This is a reference to the proverb "The walls have ears."

HIPPOLYTA

210   This is the silliest stuff that ever I heard.

This is the silliest stuff I've ever heard.

THESEUS

The best in this kind are but shadows; and the worst
are no worse, if imagination amend them.

The best actors are just representations of people, and the worst aren't any worse, if you just let imagination help them out.

HIPPOLYTA

It must be your imagination then, and not theirs.

Then it's going to have to be your imagination, not theirs.

THESEUS

If we imagine no worse of them than they of
215   themselves, they may pass for excellent men. Here
come two noble beasts in, a man and a lion.

If we imagine them to be no worse than they imagine themselves to be, then they will seem like excellent men. Here come two noble beasts, a man and a lion.

[Enter **LION** and **MOONSHINE**]

*[**LION** and **MOONSHINE** enter the scene]*

LION

[delivered by **Snug**]
You, ladies, you, whose gentle hearts do fear
The smallest monstrous mouse that creeps on floor,
May now perchance both quake and tremble here,
220 When lion rough in wildest rage doth roar.
Then know that I, one Snug the joiner, am
A lion-fell, nor else no lion's dam;
For, if I should as lion come in strife
Into this place, 'twere pity on my life.

*[delivered by **Snug**] You, ladies, you whose timid hearts fear the tiniest horrible mouse creeping across the floor, may quake and tremble here when a rough lion roars in his most terrible rage. So please understand that I, Snug the Joiner, am not a cruel lion or even a lioness, but am only a lion skin. For if I really were a lion and showed up here in a rage, my own life would be in danger.*

---

lion-fell: Although the word **fell** does mean "fierce" or "cruel," it also has the meaning of "hide," as in the hide of a lion, or Snug's lion costume. Either way, this is the speech the Mechanicals talked about in act 1, scene 2 that lets everyone know that Snug isn't really a lion.

THESEUS

225 A very gentle beast, of a good conscience.

A very polite animal, and one with a good conscience.

DEMETRIUS

The very best at a beast, my lord, that e'er I saw.

The best-played beast, my lord, that I've ever seen.

LYSANDER

This lion is a very fox for his valour.

This lion is as brave as a fox.

THESEUS

True; and a goose for his discretion.

True, and he has with the wisdom of a goose.

DEMETRIUS

Not so, my lord; for his valour cannot carry his
230   discretion; and the fox carries the goose.

Not really, my lord. He doesn't have enough bravery to support his wisdom, but a fox has enough strength to carry a goose.

THESEUS

His discretion, I am sure, cannot carry his valour;
for the goose carries not the fox. It is well:
leave it to his discretion, and let us listen to the moon.

And I'm sure his wisdom is insufficient to support his bravery, since a goose isn't strong enough to carry a fox. But be that as it may. Let's leave this to his wisdom, and listen to the moon.

MOONSHINE

[delivered by **Starveling**]
This lanthorn doth the horned moon present;—

*[delivered by **Starveling**] This lantern represents the horned moon.*

The "horned" moon is the crescent moon, which resembles a horn hung in the sky. In addition, lanterns in Shakespeare's day often had sides made from translucent horn rather than glass.

DEMETRIUS

235   He should have worn the horns on his head.

He should have worn the horns on his head.

worn the horns on his head: Demetrius is using the image of a cuckold, or a man whose wife has been unfaithful to him. Folktales said that a man's head would sprout horns if his wife cheated on him.

THESEUS

He is no crescent, and his horns are
invisible within the circumference.

He's not a crescent moon, so his horns must be hidden in the full moon.

MOONSHINE

This lanthorn doth the horned moon present;
Myself the man i' the moon do seem to be.

This lantern represents the crescent moon. I myself am the man in the moon.

THESEUS

240   This is the greatest error of all the rest: the man
should be put into the lanthorn. How is it else the
man i' the moon?

This is the worst mistake they've made—the man should be inside the lantern. How else can he be the man in the moon?

DEMETRIUS

He dares not come there for the candle; for, you
see, it is already in snuff.

He can't go in because of the candle. It's already so hot that it should be snuffed out.

HIPPOLYTA

245   I am aweary of this moon: would he would change!

I'm tired of this moon. If only he'd enter another phase.

THESEUS

It appears, by his small light of discretion, that
he is in the wane; but yet, in courtesy, in all
reason, we must stay the time.

*To judge by the small light of his wisdom, he is on the wane. But to be polite, we
must wait and see.*

---

he is in the wane: Theseus is saying that the moon is waning—growing smaller
as opposed to waxing, or growing fuller. In other words, the "moon," known as
the character Moonshine, has almost finished his speech. That Theseus and
Hippolyta are talking about Moonshine is evident from Hippolyta's earlier use of
the male personal pronoun ("would he would change"), since the moon normally
would have been spoken of as she.

LYSANDER

Proceed, Moon.

Go on, Moon.

MOONSHINE

250   All that I have to say, is, to tell you that the
lanthorn is the moon; I, the man in the moon; this
thorn-bush, my thorn-bush; and this dog, my dog.

*All I'm trying to say is that the lantern is the moon, I am the man in the moon, this
thorn bush is my thorn bush, and this dog is my dog.*

Poor Moonshine just wants to tell them that he's Moonshine. He's a bit rattled
by all the comments from the audience. As noted in act 3, the man in the moon
was often shown carrying a bundle of thorns.

DEMETRIUS

Why, all these should be in the lanthorn; for all
these are in the moon. But, silence! here comes Thisbe.

I'm telling you, all these things should be inside the lantern, if all these things are in the moon. But quiet! Here comes Thisbe.

[Enter **THISBE**]
*[**THISBE** enters the scene]*

THISBE

[delivered by **Flute**]
255   This is old Ninny's tomb. Where is my love?

*[delivered by **Flute**] This is old Ninny's tomb. Where is my love?*

LION

[Roaring] Oh—

*[The **LION** roars] Oh—*

[**THISBE** runs off]
*[**THISBE**, chased by the roaring **LION**, runs from the scene]*

The script of the Mechanicals' play calls for Thisbe to drop her mantle, or cape, very conspicuously onstage. For comic effect, the actor playing this role in *A Midsummer Night's Dream* can have Thisbe forget to drop her mantle—a "mistake" that would oblige Thisbe to return to the stage and drop her mantle after having already escaped the lion.

DEMETRIUS

Well roared, Lion.

Good roar, Lion.

THESEUS

Well run, Thisbe.

Good run, Thisbe.

HIPPOLYTA

260 Well shone, Moon. Truly, the moon shines with a
good grace.

Good shining, Moon. The moon really does shine nicely.

[The **LION** shakes **THISBE**'s mantle, and exit]
*[The **LION** shakes **THISBE**'s cape and leaves the scene]*

THESEUS

Well moused, Lion.

Well moused, Lion.

---

moused: Theseus is referring to the fact that the Lion has shaken Thisbe's cape
the way a cat would shake a mouse.

LYSANDER

And so the lion vanished.

And with that, the lion is gone.

DEMETRIUS

And then came Pyramus.

And here comes Pyramus.

[Enter **PYRAMUS**]
*[**PYRAMUS** enters the scene]*

PYRAMUS

[delivered by **Bottom**]
Sweet Moon, I thank thee for thy sunny beams;
265 I thank thee, Moon, for shining now so bright;
For, by thy gracious, golden, glittering gleams,
I trust to take of truest Thisby sight.
But stay, O spite!
But mark, poor knight,

270   What dreadful dole is here!
      Eyes, do you see?
      How can it be?
      O dainty duck! O dear!
      Thy mantle good,
275   What, stain'd with blood!
      Approach, ye Furies fell!
      O Fates, come, come,
      Cut thread and thrum;
      Quail, crush, conclude, and quell!

*[delivered by **Bottom**] Sweet Moon, I thank you for your sunny beams. I thank you, Moon, for shining so bright, for with your gracious, golden, glittering gleams, I'm sure I'll be able to see my faithful Thisby. But wait! Oh, what bad luck! But look, poor brave, noble me, what sorrowful sight do I see? Eyes, do you see? How can it be? Oh, dainty duck! Oh dear! Your fine cape is stained with blood! Come, dreadful Furies, strike a deadly blow! Oh Fates, come, come, and cut the thread of life. Overpower, crush, finish, and kill!*

Furies: Also known as the Angry Ones, the Furies are the avenging goddesses of Greek and Roman mythology. When they attack, nothing—not prayers, pleas, or reason—can turn their wrath aside.

Fates: In mythology, the Fates are the three goddesses who determine the path of a person's life, including its length. Clotho spins the thread of life, Lachesis decides the person's way of life and measures the life's thread, and Atropos cuts the thread of life when it is time for the person's life to end. The word ***thrum*** means the end of the warp (that is, the thread that runs vertically on a loom). Bottom, a weaver, would have been very familiar with this term.

THESEUS

280   This passion, and the death of a dear friend, would
      go near to make a man look sad.

So much emotion could almost make a man look sad, if one of his best friends happened to die at the same time.

HIPPOLYTA

Beshrew my heart, but I pity the man.

Curse me, but I feel sorry for him.

PYRAMUS

O wherefore, Nature, didst thou lions frame?
Since lion vile hath here deflower'd my dear:
285 Which is—no, no—which was the fairest dam
That lived, that loved, that liked, that look'd
with cheer.
Come, tears, confound;
Out, sword, and wound
290 The pap of Pyramus;
Ay, that left pap,
Where heart doth hop:
[Stabs himself]
Thus die I, thus, thus, thus.
Now am I dead,
295 Now am I fled;
My soul is in the sky:
Tongue, lose thy light;
Moon take thy flight:
[Exit **Moonshine**]
Now die, die, die, die, die.
[Dies]

*Oh why, Nature, did you create lions? A lion has cruelly deflowered my dear. She is—
no, no—was the fairest lady that ever lived, ever loved, liked, or looked so sweetly.
Come, tears, destroy me. Come out, sword, and wound the boob of Pyramus. Yes, the
left tit, where the heart hops around. [**PYRAMUS** stabs himself] Now I die, now, now,
now. Now I am dead. Now I am fled. My soul is in the sky. Tongue, lose your light.
Moon, take your flight. [**MOONSHINE** leaves the scene] Now, die, die, die, die, die.
[**PYRAMUS** dies]*

---

deflower'd: What Bottom actually means is that the Lion appears to have
devoured Thisbe, not taken her virginity.

pap: This is rural speech. What Bottom does here, referring to the seat of love and other lofty emotions, is replace the literary term *breast* with a word akin to *boob* or *tit*.

Tongue, lose thy light: Bottom mixes up the last two lines—he means "Tongue, take your flight," as in "Tongue, be silenced" and "Moon, lose your light," to tell the moon to go away. Luckily, Moonshine still picks up on his cue, and he leaves the scene.

Clearly, Bottom makes the absolute most of his big death scene.

DEMETRIUS

300   No die, but an ace, for him; for he is but one.

Die? For him, that would have to be the ace.

> **no die, but an ace:** A die is a cube with one to six dots marked on each of its six sides, and two such cubes are a pair of dice. Here, Demetrius deliberately distorts the meaning of Bottom's "die" in order to say that Bottom is the "ace," or that side of a die marked with just one dot.

LYSANDER

Less than an ace, man; for he is dead; he is nothing.

Less than that one dot, because now that he's dead, he's nothing at all.

THESEUS

With the help of a surgeon he might yet recover, and
prove an ass.

With a doctor's help, he could still recover and turn out to be an ass, not an ace.

> **prove an ass:** The audience knows that Bottom has already been an ass, and Shakespeare takes advantage of that knowledge by having Theseus make this pun on the word *ace*.

HIPPOLYTA

How chance Moonshine is gone before Thisbe comes
305   back and finds her lover?

How will Thisbe see her lover, now that Moonshine is gone?

THESEUS

She will find him by starlight. Here she comes; and
her passion ends the play.

She'll see him by starlight. Here she comes, and her grief will end the play.

[Re-enter **THISBE**]
*[**THISBE** reenters the scene]*

HIPPOLYTA

Methinks she should not use a long one for such a
Pyramus: I hope she will be brief.

I don't think she should be that upset over this Pyramus. I hope she'll finish up fast.

DEMETRIUS

310   A mote will turn the balance, which Pyramus, which
Thisbe, is the better; he for a man, God warrant us;
she for a woman, God bless us.

It won't take much to decide which of them is better—Pyramus, God help us, as a man, or Thisbe, God help us, as a woman.

LYSANDER

She hath spied him already with those sweet eyes.

She has already seen him with those beautiful eyes.

DEMETRIUS

And thus she moans, videlicet:—

And so the moaning begins, which is to say—

videlicet: Demetrius has slipped into Latin.

THISBE

[delivered by **Flute**]
315 Asleep, my love?
What, dead, my dove?
O Pyramus, arise!
Speak, speak. Quite dumb?
Dead, dead? A tomb
320 Must cover thy sweet eyes.
These lily lips,
This cherry nose,
These yellow cowslip cheeks,
Are gone, are gone:
325 Lovers, make moan:
His eyes were green as leeks.
O Sisters Three,
Come, come to me,
With hands as pale as milk;
330 Lay them in gore,
Since you have shore
With shears his thread of silk.
Tongue, not a word:
Come, trusty sword;
335 Come, blade, my breast imbrue:
[Stabs herself]
And, farewell, friends;
Thus Thisby ends:
Adieu, adieu, adieu.
[Dies]

*[delivered by **Flute**] Asleep, my love? What—dead, my dove? Oh, Pyramus, get up! Speak, speak! Can't you speak? Dead, dead? And now a tomb must cover your beautiful eyes. Those lips like a white lily, this nose like a cherry, these yellow cowslip cheeks are gone, gone! Moan, oh lovers! His eyes were as green as leeks. Oh, three Fates, come, come to me! Drench your milk-white hands in blood, since you have cut his life's thread. Tongue, don't speak a word! Come, trusty sword, come blade, stain*

*my breast with blood. [**THISBE** stabs herself] And farewell, friends. Now Thisby dies. Good-bye, good-bye, good-bye. [**THISBE** dies]*

---

green as leeks: Thisbe/Flute does not give the most attractive description of Pyramus—white lips, a red nose, yellow cheeks, and eyes like a leek, or a vegetable resembling a green onion.

Sisters Three: Thisbe also references the three Fates and the way they cut the thread of life.

After stabbing herself, Thisbe—like Pyramus—still manages to announce her death and slowly die.

THESEUS

Moonshine and Lion are left to bury the dead.

Moonshine and Lion will have to bury the dead.

DEMETRIUS

340   Ay, and Wall too.

Yes, and Wall, too.

BOTTOM

[Starting up] No assure you; the wall is down that parted their fathers. Will it please you to see the epilogue, or to hear a Bergomask dance between two of our company?

*[**Bottom** speaks to **Demetrius**] No, I assure you, the wall that separated their families has come down. [**Bottom** speaks to **Theseus**] Would you like to see the epilogue, or hear a Bergomask dance performed by two members of our cast?*

Bergomask: Bottom—who again breaks character to offer an unnecessary explanation—is talking about a rustic circle dance that was variously known as a Bergomask, a Bergamask, a bergamesca, and a bergamasca. It originated in the Italian town of Bergamo and was not the sort of thing that would have been seen in the palace of a duke like Theseus.

THESEUS

345   No epilogue, I pray you; for your play needs no
excuse. Never excuse; for when the players are all
dead, there needs none to be blamed. Marry, if he
that writ it had played Pyramus and hanged himself
in Thisbe's garter, it would have been a fine
350   tragedy: and so it is, truly; and very notably
discharged. But come, your Bergomask: let your
epilogue alone.

*No epilogue, please, for your play needs no excuse. Never apologize—when all the
actors are dead, there's no one left to be blamed. Indeed, if the one who wrote this
play had played the part of Pyramus and hanged himself with Thisbe's garter, it
would have been a good tragedy. So this tragedy has been performed very well. But
now, do your Bergomask dance. Forget the epilogue.*

> **your play needs no excuse:** A play's epilogue often included explanations
> and apologies to the audience for possible offenses or poor performances.
> This may also be a sly way for Theseus to say that there is no excuse for the
> Mechanicals' play.

[A dance]
[A dance is performed]

The iron tongue of midnight hath told twelve:
Lovers, to bed; 'tis almost fairy time.
355   I fear we shall out-sleep the coming morn
As much as we this night have overwatch'd.
This palpable-gross play hath well beguiled
The heavy gait of night. Sweet friends, to bed.
A fortnight hold we this solemnity,
360   In nightly revels and new jollity.

*The clock says it's midnight. Lovers, let's go to bed. It's almost fairy time. I suspect
we will sleep late tomorrow morning, since we have stayed up so late tonight. This
obviously dull play has kept us entertained through the slow hours of the evening.
Sweet friends, let's go to bed. We'll have festivities and nightly entertainments for
two weeks to celebrate our wedding.*

Theseus knows about the legends saying that the fairies come out at night. But, as we know from his earlier speeches, he doesn't believe in the supernatural world. Nevertheless, the audience does know that the fairies will be out tonight—dramatic irony again.

[Exeunt]
[Everyone leaves the scene]

[Enter **Puck**]
*[**Puck** enters the scene]*

PUCK

Now the hungry lion roars,
And the wolf behowls the moon;
Whilst the heavy ploughman snores,
All with weary task fordone.
365 Now the wasted brands do glow,
Whilst the screech-owl, screeching loud,
Puts the wretch that lies in woe
In remembrance of a shroud.
Now it is the time of night
370 That the graves all gaping wide,
Every one lets forth his sprite,
In the church-way paths to glide:
And we fairies, that do run
By the triple Hecate's team,
375 From the presence of the sun,
Following darkness like a dream,
Now are frolic: not a mouse
Shall disturb this hallow'd house:
I am sent with broom before,
380 To sweep the dust behind the door.

Now the hungry lion roars, and the wolf howls at the moon while the tired ploughman sleeps, exhausted by all his work. Now the logs have burned down to their glowing embers while the screech-owl, screeching loudly, makes the poor man who lies in pain think about his death. Now it is that time of night when all the graves open wide, letting all the spirits out to wander the paths of the churchyard. And we fairies, we who run with Hecate's team of dragons away from the sun, chasing the darkness like a dream, now we can play. I won't let a mouse disturb this blessed house. I am here to sweep the dust from behind the door.

---

the triple Hecate's team: Hecate, goddess of the night and the underworld, has three roles. In the heavens, she is Cynthia, goddess of the moon. On the Earth, she is Diana, goddess of chastity, and Proserpina, the goddess who brings the springtime. Here, Puck pictures her as the goddess of the night, driving a chariot led by dragons across the dark sky.

to sweep the dust: Robin Goodfellow was a so-called household spirit who cleaned up before the arrival of the king and the queen of the fairies.

[Enter **Oberon** and **Titania** with their **Train**]
*[**Oberon** and **Titania** enter the scene with their **Attendants**]*

OBERON

Through the house give gathering light,
By the dead and drowsy fire:
Every elf and fairy sprite
Hop as light as bird from brier;
385 And this ditty, after me,
Sing, and dance it trippingly.

Let the house be lit by the glow of the dying fire. All you elves and fairies, hop as lightly as a bird on a branch, and sing and dance this song with me.

TITANIA

First, rehearse your song by rote
To each word a warbling note:
Hand in hand, with fairy grace,
390 Will we sing, and bless this place.

First practice your song to make sure you know it by heart, and give each word its own note. Hand in hand, with our fairy grace, we will sing and bless this house.

[Song and dance]
[A song and a dance are performed]

OBERON

Now, until the break of day,
Through this house each fairy stray.
To the best bride-bed will we,
Which by us shall blessed be;
395   And the issue there create
Ever shall be fortunate.
So shall all the couples three
Ever true in loving be;
And the blots of Nature's hand
400   Shall not in their issue stand.
Never mole, hare lip, nor scar,
Nor mark prodigious, such as are
Despised in nativity,
Shall upon their children be.
405   With this field-dew consecrate,
Every fairy take his gait;
And each several chamber bless,
Through this palace, with sweet peace;
And the owner of it blest
410   Ever shall in safety rest.
Trip away; make no stay;
Meet me all by break of day.

From now until morning, let every fairy wander through this house. We will find the ducal couple's bedroom and bless their bed. Any children conceived there will always have good luck. All three of these couples will always be faithful in their love, and their children will be beautiful—no moles, harelips, scars, or large birthmarks, or anything else that might disturb the parents of a newborn, shall be found on their children. Fairies, take the dew from the fields, and use it to bless each room in this palace so that everyone in them will have peace and security. Dance away, don't wait too long, and meet me back here by dawn.

[Exeunt **Oberon**, **Titania**, and **Train**]
*[**Oberon**, **Titania**, and their **Attendants** leave the scene]*

PUCK

> If we shadows have offended,
> Think but this, and all is mended,
> 415 That you have but slumber'd here
> While these visions did appear.
> And this weak and idle theme,
> No more yielding but a dream,
> Gentles, do not reprehend:
> 420 If you pardon, we will mend:
> And, as I am an honest Puck,
> If we have unearned luck
> Now to 'scape the serpent's tongue,
> We will make amends ere long;
> 425 Else the Puck a liar call;
> So, good night unto you all.
> Give me your hands, if we be friends,
> And Robin shall restore amends.

If we actors have offended you, just think about it this way, and everything will be all right. Imagine that you've been sleeping here, and that all the visions and this silly story that you saw have been nothing but a dream. Ladies and gentlemen, don't criticize us. If you forgive us, we'll do better next time. I'm an honest Puck, so if we are lucky enough to escape your boos, we will fix it all soon enough. If not, you can call Puck a liar. So good night to you all. Applaud us if you are our friends, and in the future all will be made right.

the serpent's tongue: Puck's reference is to the hissing of an unhappy audience.

Robin shall restore amends: Although Theseus told Bottom not to recite an epilogue full of excuses and apologies, that's what Puck does here with an epilogue of his own. But Puck also asks for the audience's applause, and he promises to right any wrongs next time.

Appendix 1

Scene-by-Scene Summary of the Play

Act 1, Scene 1

Theseus, duke of Athens, is preparing for his wedding to Hippolyta, queen of the Amazons, when they are visited by Egeus, an Athenian nobleman. Egeus is angry because his daughter, Hermia, refuses to marry Demetrius, the husband he chose for her, because she is in love with Lysander. Egeus demands to be given the right to apply an old Athenian law that would let him have Hermia put to death if she continues to disobey him. But when Theseus speaks with Hermia, he gives her the choice of marrying Demetrius, being executed according to the law, or entering a religious order that requires lifelong virginity. Later, Hermia and Lysander decide to meet the following night in the forest and then run away to his aunt's house outside Athens, where they can be together. Helena, Hermia's friend, comes upon the couple, and Hermia tells Helena about her plan to run away with Lysander. Helena is in love with Demetrius, and he once professed his love to her, perhaps insincerely. But now he has fallen in love with Hermia and left Helena heartbroken and resentful of her friend. Helena decides that she will tell Demetrius about Hermia and Lysander's plan, hoping that Demetrius will appreciate her for giving him this information.

Act 1, Scene 2

A group of Athenian tradesmen—Quince, Bottom, Flute, Snout, Snug, and Starveling, known as the Mechanicals—get together to plan their performance of a play that they want to present in honor of Theseus's marriage to Hippolyta. The Mechanicals have chosen to stage an ancient tragic romance, the story of two doomed lovers, Pyramus and Thisbe. But even though they think they know what they're doing, and they think they are putting on a comedy, they show that they have little idea of how to put on a play.

Act 2, Scene 1

Oberon, king of the fairies, and Titania, queen of the fairies, run into each other in the forest. They have been arguing over a changeling boy, the child of a mortal friend of Titania's who was from India. Oberon wants the boy to be his page, but Titania won't give him up, out of loyalty to her deceased friend. Their disagreement has caused a disturbance in nature that has brought floods, changes in the climate, and illness to the mortal world. Oberon decides to send his assistant and jester—Puck, also known as Robin Goodfellow—to fetch a magic flower whose juice, when dabbed on a sleeping person's eyes, will make that person fall madly in love with the first person or thing he or she sees upon waking up. Oberon hopes that when he puts the juice on Titania's eyes, she will fall in love with something monstrous, and then he will threaten not to lift the spell unless she gives the changeling Indian boy up to him. Puck goes to get the flower, and Oberon, waiting for Puck to return, sees the pathetic Helena trailing after Demetrius, who is angry with her for following him. When Puck returns with the flower, Oberon tells him to take some of the love juice and put it on the eyes of the scornful Athenian man so he will fall in love with the poor Athenian girl who loves him. Puck agrees.

Act 2, Scene 2

Titania falls asleep in the woods, and Oberon puts the love juice from the magic flower on her eyes so that she will fall in love with the first thing she sees when she wakes up. Hermia and Lysander, exhausted from running through the woods in the dark, decide to stop and rest. Lysander tries to convince Hermia that they should sleep together, but she tells him to keep his distance. Puck discovers them, and he thinks that Lysander is the young Athenian Oberon asked him to find. He puts love juice from the flower on Lysander's eyes. Helena and Demetrius arrive, but Demetrius tells Helena that if she continues to follow him, he will do her harm. He leaves Helena standing there, and at that moment Lysander wakes up. Since Helena is the first person he sees, he falls madly in love with her. To Helena's disbelief, Lysander swears his love for her, and she runs away, with Lysander chasing after her. Hermia wakes up, alone and frightened after a nightmare in which a snake was eating her heart while Lysander sat by and did nothing, and she goes off to find him.

Act 3, Scene 1

The Mechanicals arrive in the woods to rehearse their play. They try to improve the script by adding explanatory prologues to help the audience understand that the play's action isn't real, but these efforts just promise to make the show worse. Puck sees their awful rehearsal and decides to play a trick on them—he puts an ass's head on the pompous Bottom. The rest of the Mechanicals are terrified when they see Bottom, and they run away, but Bottom has no idea why they're frightened. Titania then wakes up and sees him. Thanks to the magic juice that Oberon put on her eyes, Titania falls in love with Bottom and orders her fairies to be his servants. She then takes him off to bed.

Act 3, Scene 2

Puck is pleased with his trick, and he tells Oberon that Titania has fallen in love with a monstrous creature. Then the two of them see Hermia and Demetrius arguing, and they realize that Puck has put the love juice on the eyes of the wrong Athenian. They try to solve the problem by putting the love juice on Demetrius's eyes when he lies down to go to sleep. But things become more complicated when Helena arrives, with Lysander still in hot pursuit, and the two of them wake up Demetrius, who promptly falls in love with Helena himself. Now Hermia finally catches up with Lysander, and she can't believe that he has abandoned her for Helena, but he makes it clear that he is indeed in love with Helena. Hermia, furious, attacks Helena for stealing her man. As for Helena, she believes that the other three are conspiring to make her feel worse by acting out this scenario in which both men are in love with her. Hermia, angry because she thinks the others are insulting her, lashes out, but both men swear to defend only Helena. Oberon orders Puck to correct his mistake, and with Lysander and Demetrius on the point of a duel, Puck leads the two of them deeper and deeper into the forest, until they fall asleep. Puck then puts the juice from a different flower on Lysander's eyes to lift the spell from the flower that made him fall in love with Helena. Hermia and Helena arrive and fall asleep near the two men.

Act 4, Scene 1

Titania and her fairies fuss over Bottom, treating him like a king and trying to give him everything he wants. Bottom, since he is now partly an ass, is most interested in things like having his ears scratched and eating hay. He and Titania settle down for a nap, with Oberon hiding in the background. Puck happens along, and Oberon tells him that Titania has agreed to give up the changeling Indian boy. Oberon now lifts the love spell from Titania. She wakes up and tells Oberon that she had a dream of being in love with a monstrous creature. Oberon points Bottom out to her, showing her that it wasn't a dream. Titania is horrified by the sight of Bottom and his ass's head. Now that Oberon has what he wanted, the quarrel between the fairy king and the fairy queen is forgotten, and the two of them leave together. Bottom is still asleep, and Puck removes the ass's head from him.

Theseus, Hippolyta, and Egeus, out hunting in the woods on the morning of the wedding, stumble upon the four sleeping lovers. When they wake up, Lysander, as Oberon planned, no longer remembers loving Helena and has fallen back in love with Hermia. The four aren't sure how they got where they are, but Hermia and Lysander admit that they originally went into the forest because they were running away together. Egeus thinks that Theseus should have Lysander arrested for stealing his daughter. But Demetrius now says that he's in love again with Helena and that he was engaged to her before falling in love with Hermia. Theseus decides that no one should be punished, and that the two couples should be married along with himself and Hippolyta. They all go to Theseus's palace to get ready for the weddings.

Bottom wakes up, with vague memories of extraordinary and unexplained happenings. He rushes back to Athens to rejoin the other Mechanicals.

Act 4, Scene 2

Back in Athens, the Mechanicals are regretting the loss of Bottom and of their chance to perform in front of Theseus, who they are sure would have rewarded them handsomely for their wonderful theatrical work. Suddenly Bottom returns, and everyone is overjoyed. He tells them that he has had a strange experience and, after coyly refusing to tell them anything about it, promises to tell them everything. But he will tell them later, because it turns out that they are going to perform their play after all, and they must hurry off to get ready.

Act 5, Scene 1

The wedding ceremonies are over, and at the palace, Theseus and Hippolyta discuss the strange story told to them by the now married young lovers. Theseus dismisses it all as the nonsensical ravings of lovers, lumping lovers in with lunatics and poets. Hippolyta protests that there must be some truth to the story, since the details are so consistent. Theseus calls to Philostrate, his master of revels, and asks him to suggest some entertainment for the three couples. Philostrate shows him a list of possibilities, but Theseus isn't interested in any of the offerings until he sees the description of the Mechanicals' play. Philostrate warns him that the play is awful, but Theseus thinks it will be fun. Hippolyta doesn't think it's right to watch a play just to make fun of it, but Theseus explains that they will be making the Mechanicals happy by letting them perform and that the audience can enjoy the play if only because the cast members will be performing with sincerity and doing their best.

The Mechanicals' play is, as predicted, a disaster, marred by overacting and many other mistakes. But the Athenians keep themselves amused by making fun of the play as it progresses. At the end of the Mechanicals' play within the play, Bottom offers the audience the choice of an epilogue or a dance, and Theseus selects the dance to be performed. When the dance is over, the couples go off to bed.

After everyone has gone, the fairies arrive. Oberon orders the fairies to go through the palace and bless each room so that the three marriages and the three couples' future children will be happy. After the rest of the fairies leave, Puck delivers an epilogue, telling the members of the audience that if they didn't like the play, they should just consider it to have been a dream. He asks forgiveness for anything that may have offended the audience, and he asks for applause if the audience liked the play.

Appendix 2

Cast of Characters

The Athenians

THESEUS

The highest-born mortal in the play, Theseus is presented as the voice of reason. He appears only at the beginning and the end of the play, staying out of the nighttime shenanigans in the forest. When the subject of fantasy and dreams comes up, Theseus dismisses them scornfully in his "lunatics, lovers, and poets" speech (act 5, scene 1). His staid, reserved appearance may not tell the whole story, though—in act 2, scene 2, Oberon baits Titania, slyly bringing up her past with Theseus and Theseus's own past with a number of other women. At the end of the play, Theseus loftily lectures Hippolyta about how allowing the Mechanicals to perform their play, no matter how badly, is an act of generosity and sincere appreciation. Yet when the play is performed, he indulges in making fun of the players, just as he said he would not. Theseus's calm exterior hides a heart of mischief.

Theseus is the one who is asked to handle the problems between Egeus, who wants Hermia executed for disobeying him, and Hermia, who wants to disobey her father without any consequences. Theseus offers a middle ground to Hermia—a life of virginity in a religious order. This seems like a generous offer on the surface, but Theseus's description of that life makes it seem as if Hermia would be choosing a living death. In the end, though, even if Theseus does represent the harshness of the law, he understands order—when he sees the well-matched pairs that emerge from the night in the forest, he does not continue to fight true love but instead decrees that they should all be married. In Theseus's Athens, balance makes more sense than a hard line.

HIPPOLYTA

Like her soon-to-be husband, Theseus, Hippolyta also stays out of the overheated adventures in the forest, appearing only at the beginning of the play and at the end of the long, fantastic night. Hippolyta was queen of the Amazons, but it's hard to reconcile the placid woman idly commenting on the action with the image of the onetime leader of a race of woman warriors. Again, though, as is the case with Theseus, there are hints of a more adventurous past when Titania snidely refers to Hippolyta as Oberon's "bouncing Amazon," "mistress," and "warrior love" (act 2, scene 2). The idea of a warrior queen cavorting with a fairy king seems a far cry from the play's Hippolyta, who is most notable onstage for her mild willingness to consider the truth of the young lovers' story about their night in the forest and her snarkiness during the Mechanicals' play.

It has been suggested that this representation of Hippolyta has a deeper purpose. Queen Elizabeth was often portrayed as a warrior queen herself, but her decision to stay unmarried and childless, with no named heir, excited a great deal of anxiety as the sixteenth century came to a close. People were worried about who would rule England after her death. The portrayal of a fiercely independent queen who was duly tamed by an appropriate king could be seen as Elizabethan wish fulfillment. Theseus tells Hippolyta that he won her with his sword and caused her injury in the process, and Hippolyta seems fine with that.

HERMIA

From the very first moment we see her, Hermia is defined by a characteristic that some may call strength and others may call mere stubbornness. With her father demanding the right to have her executed, Hermia jumps into the conversation and addresses Theseus, the most powerful man in Athens. She protests that Lysander is just as good a man as Demetrius and then swears to Theseus that she will die a virgin rather than submit to Demetrius, a man she does not want. She half apologizes to Theseus, saying that such boldness does not help a girl's reputation, but Hermia is bold. She won't let social niceties bury her true character or her belief that she has the right to be with the one she loves. She doesn't let love get in the way of good sense, though—when Lysander tries to talk her into letting him sleep with her in the forest, she not only refuses to give in but does it in a way that makes Lysander meekly retreat.

Hermia and Lysander have a playful conversation (act 1, scene 1) about how true love is always tested, but Hermia is the only one who is really put through the grinder. When Lysander abandons her without explanation, she doesn't mope but just goes after him. He tells her that he no longer loves her, but she refuses to give up on him. Hermia can be played as a spoiled brat, one who can't believe that someone would stop loving her, or as a girl who believes in her love and is willing to fight for it. Either way, Helena's warning about her (act 3, scene 2) remains true: "Though she be but little, she is fierce."

LYSANDER

Egeus's angry description of Lysander as a scam artist who has bewitched his daughter actually makes Lysander sound more like a young man who has fully bought into the hearts-and-flowers version of romance. He gives Hermia rings, toys, bracelets made from his hair, and candy, and then he tops it all off by standing under her window and singing love songs. Lysander is knowledgeable about the history of romance, too. He's the one who says, "The course of true love never did run smooth" (act 1, scene 1), and then he cites all the things—age differences, family issues, differences in social class, war, illness—that keep lovers apart in classic stories of romance. Despite all his passion, Lysander does recognize the fleeting nature of love, comparing it to lightning (act 1, scene 1) in a way that mirrors what Juliet says in act 2, scene 2 of *Romeo and Juliet*, which Shakespeare was writing around the same time:

> Well, do not swear: although I joy in thee,
> I have no joy of this contract to-night:
> It is too rash, too unadvised, too sudden;
> Too like the lightning, which doth cease to be
> Ere one can say "It lightens." Sweet, good night!

Though his efforts to win Hermia are intense, there is a lightheartedness about Lysander. When Demetrius insists that Hermia should give in and marry him, since he is her father's choice, Lysander tells Demetrius, in effect, "If he likes you so much, why don't you marry him?" Even his speech about the difficulties of love comes as part of a pep talk to Hermia—everything may seem awful, but he says that this is par for the course for lovers, and if they just play their parts, their love will triumph in the end.

Lysander seems so happy and committed to Hermia that it's doubly startling when he not only turns his affections to Helena but also behaves cruelly toward Hermia. Although this is the result of enchantment, it serves a larger point that Shakespeare is making—love is so strange and uncontrollable that you can be totally in love with one person today and head over heels with someone else tomorrow. Love is indeed like lightning, quick and bright, ending in confusion.

HELENA

Not one of the four Athenian lovers is a fully drawn character. Each of them has only a few definable traits, and the four of them don't grow or change during the play. But

Helena is probably the one audiences get to know best because she speaks at length more than the others. That's not always to her benefit, though—from her first entrance (act 1, scene 1), Helena is mopey and insecure, complaining on the one hand that everything would be fine if she looked like Hermia, and insisting on the other that she is just as pretty but that Demetrius can't see it because "Love looks not with the eyes, but with the mind." She works herself into such a state of self-doubt that when Demetrius does swear his love to her, she can't accept it and is convinced that his declaration is part of an elaborate joke created to make her feel bad (she is right, however, to be suspicious of Lysander's sudden over-the-top infatuation with her). Even when Demetrius confesses that he loved her before he loved Hermia and now wants to return to her, and even when Theseus decides that all the couples should be wed, Helena can't accept that she has what she wants. She is unsure of it all and can't quite believe that she really has Demetrius—and, given that he has returned to her by way of a magic spell, maybe she's right to feel that something is not quite right.

Perhaps, though, Helena just understands Shakespeare's message about love better than anyone else. Love can be frustrating and cruel, making you love someone who doesn't love you. It can make you do foolish things, like giving away your friend's secrets in order to win the guy who's ignoring you. It is blind, covering one person's faults and another's virtues. It is inconstant, coming and going from one person to another as if it were something controlled by mischievous fairies.

DEMETRIUS

It's hard for Demetrius to make a good impression in *A Midsummer Night's Dream*. Lysander romances Hermia with gifts and love songs, but Demetrius bluntly tells her to come with him, and he tells Lysander with equal bluntness to give up any right that he's crazy enough to think he has to Hermia. Demetrius's position is that Hermia should marry him simply because her father has chosen him, not because he loves her more than Lysander does. And then we find out that Demetrius was seeing Helena before but dropped her to pursue Hermia. When Egeus tells Lysander that Hermia, as his daughter, belongs to him, and that he is passing this possession on to Demetrius, there is a hint that Demetrius may have switched his interest to Hermia because Egeus plans to settle an inheritance on whoever becomes his future son-in-law.

Demetrius doesn't come off well in his interactions with Helena, either. Granted, she makes herself hard to love by constantly throwing herself at Demetrius in an embarrassing way, but he is incredibly cruel to her. The first time we see them together, he tells her to go away, and he says he's basically sick of looking at her. He then tells her that he plans to leave her in the woods to be eaten by wild beasts, and that if she tries to follow him again, he'll kill her. It's hard to understand what Helena sees in Demetrius. Then again, this may be just another illustration of Shakespeare's idea about love. It is blind indeed.

EGEUS

Like Lord Capulet in *Romeo and Juliet* and Brabantio in *Othello*, Egeus is an angry father who can't believe that Hermia, his daughter, is making such bad choices in love. Egeus represents practical age versus passionate youth. He feels that he's made a reasonable choice of husband for his daughter and can't understand why she refuses to listen to him. As for Hermia herself, she can't understand why her father doesn't care that she's not in love with Demetrius. Egeus is so convinced of his right to use Hermia in any way he pleases that he's willing to have her executed rather than give in to her wishes. Egeus has no use for love. He's all about what's practical and what makes sense to him.

PHILOSTRATE

As party planner for Theseus, Philostrate is responsible for finding entertainment on Theseus's wedding day. If Theseus and Hippolyta can be seen as mortal-world versions of Oberon and Titania, then Philostrate's counterpart is Puck, who acts as Oberon's chief entertainer. But whereas Puck is wild and unpredictable, Philostrate is anxious and careful—he does try to warn Theseus away from the Mechanicals' awful play. And it's the audience's good luck, our good luck, that Theseus doesn't take his advice.

The Fairies

OBERON

Theseus is the leader of the play's mortal world, and Oberon is the ruler of its fairy world. But Oberon, unlike the calm, rational Theseus, is moody, demanding, jealous, and petty. And yet the two of them do have something in common: Titania points out that Oberon had a fling with Hippolyta, Theseus's bride-to-be. And not just with Hippolyta, as Titania notes—Oberon's lovers have ranged from a country girl to the goddess of the dawn. In fact, Oberon is a character who fits the theme of love's inconstancy, since he seems perfectly willing to turn his fairy powers to the business of picking up women and letting them drop again.

The one thing Oberon wants, though, is Titania's love and full attention, which he feels she's been giving away to the changeling boy. So he pulls a power play and demands that Titania give him the boy. Oberon says he wants the boy to be his servant, but it's clear that he really just wants the boy because Titania loves him. When Titania complains that Oberon's jealousy and his interruptions of her fairy rites have thrown the mortal world into chaos, Oberon has the solution: "Give me that boy" (act 2, scene 1). Finally, when all else has failed, Oberon decides that he'll not only get the boy by using magic to trick Titania, he'll also make it a trick that will humiliate her.

In spite of his apparently nasty streak, Oberon has the heart of a true romantic. When he sees Demetrius's cruelty to Helena, he feels sorry for her and decides to help her by telling Puck to use the magic flower to make Demetrius fall in love with her. Puck, of course, mistakes Lysander for Demetrius and is amused by the blunder, but the ensuing disaster angers Oberon, who goes out of his way to try to bring the right couples together. Although Theseus is the one who decides to bypass the law (and Egeus's demands) by allowing the two couples to be married, it's Oberon who does the work of making sure that everyone is happily in love.

TITANIA

When we first meet Titania, she is proud, strong, and willing to speak her mind. She confronts Oberon directly about the trouble he's caused the world because of his dispute with her over the changeling boy. Oberon asks her, rhetorically, "Am not I thy lord?" Titania sarcastically replies, "Then I must be thy lady," and she tears into him about his many affairs (act 2, scene 1). But Oberon quickly points out that she hasn't exactly been moping around at home (or in a tiny bed of flowers), and he alludes to her affair with Theseus, which may have interfered with the Athenian's other loves.

After that strong first impression, it's all the more startling when Oberon enchants Titania with the magic flower's love juice and she becomes besotted with Bottom, the ass-headed country bumpkin. With her first look at Bottom, Titania illustrates all of Shakespeare's ideas about love in the play—that we have no power over love, that love makes us fools, and that love is blind. Titania is eventually returned to her normal self, but only after showing that she's as idiotic as anyone else when it comes to love, and only after giving up, with astonishing ease, the boy she protected so fiercely until she got distracted by her love for Bottom.

PUCK (ROBIN GOODFELLOW)

Puck is a classic trickster found not just in English folklore but in the folktales and myths of many other cultures as well. He is responsible for much of the play's action. As he describes his role with the fairy king, "I jest to Oberon, and make him smile" (act 2, scene 1). But Oberon entrusts Puck with the important task of using the magic flower to help Helena. Puck tries to do as he is asked, but when he and Oberon discover that Puck has made a big mistake, Puck just shrugs it off. He doesn't really care if someone gets hurt, as long as he is entertained. In that sense, he embodies the wildness of untamed nature, which also doesn't care whether human beings are happy or sad. And, like nature, he is constantly changing and unpredictable. He just does what he does—in the moment, without a care, and with no thought to the consequences.

Puck interacts with the Athenians, the Mechanicals, and of course, the fairies, and in this way he is the link that ties the three groups of characters together. As such, he also helps connect the audience to all the play's characters and stories, showing how the complicated pieces fall into place and meet up with each other. It's no wonder, then, that Puck is the one who delivers the epilogue, asking the audience to forgive any offenses. But he also reminds the members of the audience that if they dislike what they have just seen, they can easily dismiss the play as nothing more than shadows and dreams. He provides the final connection between the audience and the cast of the actual play, asking for the applause that the actors want in exchange for the night's entertainment.

PEASEBLOSSOM, MUSTARDSEED, MOTH, AND COBWEB

The fairies who attend to Titania, and who follow her orders to give Bottom everything he wants, have names meant to signify their tiny size and their delicacy.

THE CHANGELING BOY

He is never seen, but the changeling boy is one of the most important characters in the play. Oberon's jealous demand for Titania to give him the boy and her refusal to hand over the child of her dead friend have a negative effect on the mortal world and sets off the whole chain of mix-ups when Oberon decides to obtain the boy by playing a trick with a magic flower.

The Mechanicals

BOTTOM

The weaver at the center of this troupe of amateur actors is boastful, overconfident, misinformed, childish, attention-hungry, prone to verbal mistakes, completely oblivious to all his faults—and it all adds up to a character audiences love to laugh at, and a character actors love to play.

Bottom helps define the play's theme of transformation. Puck puts an ass's head on Bottom to make a fool of him and to make a fool of Titania. But Bottom's transformation works on several levels. To anyone watching, he seems to have been turned into a monstrous creature, but he's completely unaware of the change, and he remains his usual confident self. Bottom has been transformed on the outside, but if he hasn't been transformed on the inside, has he really been transformed at all? One way to approach that question is to note that, because Bottom already has the personality of an ass, it's hard to argue that a transformation actually has occurred. Luckily for the audience, he still looks funny, and he adds dramatic irony to the humor when he charges his friends (act 3, scene 1) with trying to make an ass out of him, as he stands there wearing the head of an ass.

Despite all his bad qualities, Bottom's enthusiasm and his good heart always shine through. He sincerely wants the Mechanicals to put on a good play, and he's sure he knows just how to do it—by making himself the center of everything. In his bumbling way, he seems to care about the other members of the group, who are all genuinely excited when he returns from the woods. His blissful ease at falling into the fairy world gives him an almost childlike quality. Of course, it's also true that a beautiful fairy queen is in love with him, while fairies attend to his every desire. And it all makes sense to Bottom. He shows the audience that the gap between the mortal world and the fairy world is not a large one for those who are openhearted.

QUINCE

Quince, the carpenter, is the closest thing the Mechanicals have to a director (a title that didn't exist in Elizabethan theater). He has the difficult task of organizing this group of total amateurs while also controlling Bottom's giant ego. He is confident enough to be the boss during rehearsals, but when he has to step up and deliver the play's prologue to a live audience, he chokes, turning it into a comic disaster of misplaced punctuation and terrible writing.

FLUTE

At first horrified when he is asked to play a woman, Flute, the bellows mender, comes through at showtime. In fact, if the length of Thisbe's monologue and slow death (act 5, scene 1) is any indication ("Adieu, adieu, adieu"), it's possible that once Flute puts on the dress and takes the stage, he rather enjoys himself.

SNOUT

Initially cast as Pyramus's father, Snout, the tinker, takes the role of the wall that separates Pyramus and Thisbe. Not only does he stand there as the wall, he also uses two fingers to create the hole through which the two lovers whisper to each other. Snout seems very proud of his part, convinced that he's involved in something important.

STARVELING

The tailor, originally assigned the role of Thisbe's mother, instead takes the part of Moonshine, once the Mechanicals have become convinced that having moonshine will be very, very important to the audience. The pained Starveling, mercilessly heckled by the noble Athenians, struggles to get through his few lines.

SNUG

Poor Snug, the joiner, introduces himself by asking to have the script for the Lion's part as soon as possible because, as he puts it, "I am slow of study" (act 1, scene 2). He then shows his gentleness by his concern for the temperaments of the ladies in the audience, who he thinks may be frightened if they believe he's a real lion. Nevertheless, to judge from the reactions of the Athenians in act 5, scene 1 ("Well roared, Lion"), when the time comes for him to roar and chase Thisbe, the gentle Snug turns into a total beast.

Appendix 3

The Play's Major Themes

Love as Madness

In *Romeo and Juliet*, Shakespeare asks audiences to believe that two teenagers can fall truly, madly, deeply in love at first sight, with a love so strong that it's worth dying for. In *A Midsummer Night's Dream*, written about the same time, Shakespeare pokes fun at the idea of this kind of love, suggesting that it's nothing more than a mad fever directed by the games of fairies.

In act 1, scene 1, Lysander says, "The course of true love never did run smooth," and indeed it does not for any of the lovers. Theseus and Hippolyta may seem like a placid, happy couple, but in the opening scene Theseus reminds his bride-to-be that he "woo'd" her by way of the sword and won her in battle. Lysander and Hermia are being kept apart by her father. Demetrius can't win Hermia's heart, and Helena loves the indifferent Demetrius. Titania and Oberon put their marriage—and the entire world—at risk because of a petty fight over a little boy, and the play that a group of Athenian tradesmen decide to put on tells the story of a love that ends tragically. The only courtship that goes smoothly is the one between Titania and the ass-headed Bottom, and that, of course is the result of a magic spell, forgotten as soon as the spell is lifted.

Oberon initially asks Puck to fetch the magic flower with the love juice in order to play a prank on Titania and make her fall in love with some monster (as Bottom with his ass's head turns out to be). But then Oberon tries to put the magic flower's juice to a more serious purpose—helping the brokenhearted Helena. That the same flower can be asked to do such seemingly different things—cause mischief and create true love—suggests that maybe the two aren't that far apart and that love is ridiculous. Titania falling in love with a country bumpkin who has the head of an ass is as silly as a girl chasing after a boy who's in love with someone else. Love makes people do stupid things, as when Helena decides to tell Demetrius about Hermia's plan to run away, in the hope that this disclosure will make Demetrius appreciate her. Love can make you happy, like Hermia, or unhappy, like Helena. It causes chaos as people pursue it.

Shakespeare's use of the flower's magic juice to make people fall in and out of love so quickly shows how little control people have over love, and how fleeting and strange it can be. In the end, the couples are all brought together, but this resolution depends on enchantment for at least two of them—Titania, tricked into giving up her changeling boy to make Oberon happy, and Demetrius, left under the spell of the magic flower to bring order to the Athenian couples. Is love that comes about through enchantment any less valid, happy, or long-lasting than the kind that comes about naturally? Shakespeare suggests that there really isn't much difference.

Love as Conflict

Love in *A Midsummer Night's Dream* isn't just about madness. It is also presented as a battle, a movement from conflict to harmony. Theseus and Hippolyta, the first couple we meet, have already experienced conflict (Theseus's admission, "I woo'd thee with my sword," in act 1, scene 1), and now, with their marriage just a few days away, they are on their way to harmony. Hermia is in conflict with her father over her love for Lysander. Helena is battling Demetrius's disdain for her, and Demetrius is trying to fend her off. Oberon and Titania are in the middle of a serious conflict that has turned the world upside down. Once Oberon has Puck put the magic juice on Lysander's eyes, a happy couple is thrown into turmoil as Lysander abandons Hermia for Helena, who later is chased after by Demetrius as well. While Lysander and Demetrius fight over Helena, loving her only because of a magic spell, Hermia is left alone to fight for a love that she knows is real and true. In act 1, scene 1, Lysander tells Hermia, "The course of true love never did run smooth," and Hermia learns this lesson more painfully than anyone else in the play. In fact, Bottom and Titania are the only couple with a smooth courtship, but their love, also the product of enchantment, comes and goes so quickly that Bottom is sure it was a dream. Shakespeare may be warning hopeful lovers that love is easy only in dreams.

By the end of the play, all four couples have found happiness. It comes honestly to Hermia and Lysander, and to Theseus and Hippolyta, all of whom have had their love tested. By contrast, a bit of deception aids the resolution between Oberon and Titania, and between Demetrius and Helena. Maybe the message here is that the secret of a harmonious relationship is a little magic.

Nature

Strange things happen in the forest. In another of Shakespeare's comedies, *As You Like It*, and in *A Midsummer Night's Dream*, the forest is a place where the rules have changed and where familiar people are no longer quite what they seemed to be. As soon as Lysander and Hermia enter the woods, Lysander ceases being Hermia's respectful true love and becomes a man who presses her for sexual intimacy. Hermia goes from being the most popular girl to being the least popular girl, and the Mechanicals are turned from craftsmen into actors. Mischievous fairies lurk in the dark, playing tricks, and everyone— fairies and mortals alike—is constantly overcome by the need to sleep.

The only thing more powerful than the natural world is Titania's and Oberon's anger with each other, which has thrown nature out of balance. Nature can be wonderful, as in the delights that Titania offers Bottom in act 3, scene 1: "Feed him with apricoks and dewberries, / With purple grapes, green figs, and mulberries; / The honey-bags steal from the humble-bees." It also can terrify, as Puck shows in the same act and scene, where he lists the things he can do to frighten human beings: "I'll follow you, I'll lead you about a round, / Through bog, through bush, through brake, through brier: / Sometime a horse I'll be, sometime a hound, / A hog, a headless bear, sometime a fire." Puck is not trying to scare the Mechanicals by conjuring goblins and ghosts; he chooses ordinary things from nature instead. If nature offers the best of the world, it also offers the worst.

In *A Midsummer Night's Dream*, nature and the natural world represent the true character of human beings, uninhibited by any rules of society. The events of the play couldn't happen within the civilized walls of Athens. Lysander wouldn't try to seduce Hermia in her father's house, and Helena and Hermia wouldn't get into a catfight in the streets of the city. The Mechanicals go to the forest because it's the only place where they feel free to rehearse their play. Nature is wild and uncontrollable, but it allows the truth to come out, and the natural world is the place where the business of the play can be accomplished.

Transformation

A Midsummer Night's Dream is filled with transformations both physical and emotional, magical as well as natural. For example, Helena is transformed by her desperate chase after love—at the beginning of the play, she insists that everyone in Athens thinks she is just as pretty as Hermia, but when she finds herself beaten down by her pursuit, she finds it impossible to believe that even one man, let alone two, could be in love with her. Magic transforms Demetrius and Lysander from youths who wouldn't give Helena a second glance to lovers who are willing to fight to the death for her. The Mechanicals try not only to transform themselves into the characters they portray in their play but also to elevate themselves to another class altogether, that of genteel actors fit to perform for nobles and worthy of being rewarded for their performance. Titania is changed from an imperious, confident queen to a fool who caresses a man sporting a donkey's head. Bottom is transformed from a human to a half man, half beast.

But how much of a transformation is that last example? In his scenes, both as himself and as the ass-headed man, Bottom shows that he is indeed an ass. Is he transformed, or is he just physically showing the world his true self for a little while? These transformations may not be as extreme as they seem, Shakespeare suggests. Helena is just showing the insecurity that lurks inside. Lysander and Demetrius may be showing the inconstancy of the love they claim to feel so deeply. Titania shows that inside everyone lurks a fool for love. The Mechanicals, with their good hearts and their sincerity, may be just as worthy of respect as any of the nobles. In this play, transformation may be less about characters turning into people or things they are not than about their gaining access to other parts of themselves.

Appearances and Reality

In *A Midsummer Night's Dream*, there is often a huge gap between what people think they see, what others see, and what is real. Egeus sees Hermia as a bad daughter and Lysander as a troublemaker who has used magic to make Egeus's child disobey him. Hermia and Lysander see themselves as good people in love. Helena sees Demetrius as the most wonderful young man in Athens, but audiences can easily see him as a smug, mean-spirited jerk. The Mechanicals, especially Bottom, think of themselves as competent actors, but the reality—the fact that they are unbelievably incompetent—is plain to everyone else. When they begin to rehearse their play, the Mechanicals decide that they need to give a series of prologues that will alert the audience to what is not real (the lion, the deaths of Pyramus and Thisbe). Titania believes that the ass-headed Bottom is the most beautiful creature in the world, and Bottom, perhaps most astonishingly of all, sees no gap between his real appearance and his perception of himself.

Sometimes appearances match reality, but in such an incredible way that the characters can't really believe what they're seeing, and no one is quite sure what has happened. For example, in act 4, scene 1, Titania wakes up and says, "My Oberon! what visions have I seen! / Methought I was enamour'd of an ass," and we know that what she saw was indeed real. The same thing occurs a little while later, when Bottom wakes up and says, "I have had a most rare / vision. I have had a dream, past the wit of man to / say what dream it was." Once again we know that what appeared to be absurdly unreal was actually real. Demetrius explains that when he was in love with Hermia, it was as if he was under the spell of some sickness, and yet we know that he is in love with Helena precisely because of a magic spell.

But the discrepancy between appearances and reality culminates in the Mechanicals' play. The Mechanicals are constantly worried that the audience—sophisticated Athenian nobles—won't recognize what is real and what is not. They insert prologues that explain that no one really dies onstage and that the lion is not real. When the Athenians make jokes about the action in the play, the Mechanicals take them literally and break character to tell them what is real and what is not. The theater is shown as a place where the line between appearances and reality is blurred as audiences are asked to suspend their beliefs about the real world, but the down-to-earth Mechanicals are determined to keep that line clear.

The gap between appearances and reality is one of Shakespeare's most common themes—in *Twelfth Night* and *As You Like It*, where handsome boys are girls in disguise; in *Hamlet*, where courtly appearances conceal lies and deceit; in *Macbeth*, where the title character and his wife are so paranoid that they cannot trust what they see with their own eyes. In *A Midsummer Night's Dream*, the line between what characters think they see and what they really see may be blurry, but at least that line leads them to a happy ending.

Sleep and Dreams

Even today, dreams aren't well understood—they're messy, chaotic, wonderful, terrifying, enlightening, and baffling. No wonder, then, that the characters in *A Midsummer Night's Dream* have to use the idea of dreams to explain what's happened to them.

The first dream that occurs in the play is the only one that's a real, natural dream—the startling nightmare about the snake eating her heart that wakes Hermia up at the end of act 2, scene 1. But even though this is a dream, the vision it presents of a snake attacking her while Lysander sits by doing nothing turns out to be an excellent reflection of reality, since Lysander is about to betray her.

For the rest of the play, the characters go through all kinds of wild experiences, so strange that the only way they can handle them is to perceive them as dreams. And in act 2, scene 3, Oberon ensures that this is exactly what will happen when he produces the second magic flower and explains to Puck that, after its juice is placed on the lovers' eyes, they will wake up and think that everything they've seen and experienced was a dream. But Titania isn't so lucky—when she wakes up, she says that she has had a horrible dream in which she was in love with an ass, and Oberon immediately shows her Bottom, the evidence that what she thinks was a dream is in fact real. As for Bottom, he wakes up and is convinced that everything he saw in his mind was a dream, a "most rare vision."

And yet Bottom is not horrified or confused. Instead, he seems to be delighted by what he has imagined, and he suggests that it will make wonderful material for a poem: "I will get Peter Quince to write a ballad of / this dream: it shall be called 'Bottom's Dream,' / because it hath no bottom" (act 4, scene 1). No doubt the thought that dreams can be something to write about has crossed the minds of many poets and writers throughout the ages, and the same thought may have occurred to Shakespeare.

Theseus throws the strange ideas found in dreams into the same category as madness, along with the visions of "the lunatic, the lover and the poet" (act 5, scene 1). He says he never believes the nonsense spouted by these types of dreamers, but Hippolyta argues that the four lovers' stories are so consistent that there must be something to it. Did they really experience what appeared to take place, and are they now only imagining that they were dreaming, as Oberon said they would do? Or did one of them perhaps dream those events, with the others coming more and more to believe them the more the story was repeated? We aren't given a definitive answer. Instead, we're left to conclude that the weirdest events have something of the dream in them, and that the weirdest dream may contain something of reality.

Appendix 4

About William Shakespeare

Shakespeare the playwright is well known to us, but Shakespeare the man remains something of a mystery. We know astonishingly little about him. We have his plays, of course, and a number of public records, such as those involving his birth, his marriage, and his lawsuits. (Thanks to the few records that do exist, we know that Shakespeare was a businessman—and that he wasn't shy about going after people who owed him money.) But if he left any letters behind, no one has found them, even though many people have been looking.

Here's what we do know: William Shakespeare was baptized on April 26, 1564, in Stratford-on-Avon, a town a couple of days' ride from London. Children were typically baptized three days after they were born, so it's likely that Shakespeare was born on April 23 of that year. His father, John, was a glovemaker, a leather tanner, and a property owner. His mother, Mary Arden, came from a well-regarded family. William was the third of the couple's eight children. There aren't any records absolutely proving that young William went to school, but it would have been common for a boy of his social class to attend the local grammar school, and his work does reflect the basic Greek and Latin that schoolboys would have been taught in those days.

After the record of his baptism, the next one we have for him shows that in 1582, at the age of eighteen, he married Anne Hathaway, the twenty-six-year-old daughter of a well-off Stratford farmer. William and Anne's first child, Susannah, was born six months later, so it's likely that they got married because Anne was pregnant. Three years after Susannah was born, Anne gave birth to fraternal twins, Judith and Hamnet (Hamnet died when the twins were eleven).

All public mention of William Shakespeare now disappears until 1592, when his name begins to pop up in the London theater world. In other words, at some point Shakespeare must have decided that he wanted to be an actor and set off for London to make his dream come true—a choice that probably upset his family because, then as now, it was hard to make a living in the theater. To make matters worse, actors weren't even considered respectable members of the community. But as we know now, Shakespeare was one of the lucky few.

Like other performers of his time, Shakespeare not only acted on the stage but also wrote plays in which he appeared. His plays began to be staged in 1592. In 1594, he cofounded the Lord Chamberlain's Men, a theater company supported by Henry Carey, lord chamberlain to Queen Elizabeth I. In 1603, the company's name was changed to the King's Men, after Elizabeth died and King James I succeeded to the throne and became the new patron. Having this kind of support gave the company a significant advantage over other troupes of actors and writers, who had to scramble not just for money but also for time to devote to the theater. It's not unlikely that royal support is what made it possible for Shakespeare to write as many plays as he did.

The King's Men became popular with the nobility, for whom the company often gave private command performances, as well as with regular London theatergoers. In particular, Shakespeare's plays became so well known that a number of printers collected the scripts and sold them as books—a very unusual degree of success in those days. As if writing and performing didn't keep him busy enough, Shakespeare also served as the company's managing partner and handled most of its business affairs. By 1597 he had made enough money to buy a large house in Stratford, although it's likely that he continued to spend most of his time in London. But in 1611 he retired from the London theater and returned to Stratford, where he probably lived the life of a wealthy country gentleman until April 1616, when he died.

So what is it that makes Shakespeare so special? Why are his plays considered some of the greatest works of dramatic art ever produced?

One explanation is that Shakespeare's plays have a little of everything—high drama, low comedy, action. He knew just how to reach an audience. His darkest dramas have moments of humor, and his comedies have moments of deep emotion. In short, his plays are hugely entertaining.

But there are plenty of other entertaining plays from that time, so something else must make Shakespeare stand out. Indeed there is—it's his remarkable use of language. Shakespeare wrote some of the most beautiful poetry ever composed in the English language. There are lines and phrases from his plays that people quote today in ordinary conversation, often without even realizing that they're quoting Shakespeare.

Then there's what Shakespeare wrote about. The raw material of his plays is not just hopes and dreams, war and power struggles, but also the human emotions that have always been the common language of people everywhere, in all times, right up to our own time: ambition, fear, hatred, envy, self-doubt, and—most of all, as in *A Midsummer Night's Dream*—love.

CPSIA information can be obtained
at www.ICGtesting.com
Printed in the USA
BVOW08s2343030317
477767BV00001B/8/P